D0724447

62

Comedy
DUET
Scenes
for
Teens

*More real-life
situations for
laughter*

LAURIE
ALLEN

WITHDRAWN
MANITOWOC PUBLIC LIBRARY
FROM
MANITOWOC   2013
PUBLIC LIBRARY
MANITOWOC, WI 54220

mp
MERIWETHER PUBLISHING LTD.
Colorado Springs, Colorado

Meriwether Publishing Ltd., Publisher
PO Box 7710
Colorado Springs, CO 80933-7710

www.meriwether.com

Editor: Theodore O. Zapel
Assistant editor: Amy Hammelev
Cover design: Jan Melvin

© Copyright MMXII Meriwether Publishing Ltd.
Printed in the United States of America
First Edition

All rights reserved. All rights, including professional, motion picture, radio broadcasting, television, video or sound taping, all other forms of mechanical or electronic reproductions such as information storage and retrieval systems and photocopying, and the rights of translation into foreign languages, are strictly reserved by the publisher, Meriwether Publishing Ltd. Any inquiries concerning these rights should be directed to the publisher (address above).

The rights to unlimited amateur performances of these duet scenes at one location are granted with the purchase of this book. For performances at another location, a royalty fee of $5.00 per duet scene per location must be remitted to Meriwether Publishing Ltd. (address above).

Permission to reproduce copies of the scenes included in this text is granted to amateur groups with the purchase of this book. All copies must display the copyright notice indicated on this page. Copies of these scenes and amateur performance rights are for the purchaser and purchasing organization only. These rights may not be sold or transferred to any third party.

NOTICE FOR PROFESSIONAL PRODUCTION
For any form of non-amateur presentation (professional stage, radio, video, or television), permission must be obtained in writing from the publisher, Meriwether Publishing, Ltd., (address above).

Library of Congress Cataloging-in-Publication Data

Allen, Laurie, 1962-
  62 comedy duet scenes for teens / by Laurie Allen. -- 1st ed.
    p. cm.
  ISBN 978-1-56608-186-3
  1. Young adult drama, American. 2. Comedy sketches. 3. Teenagers--Drama.
I. Title. II. Title: Sixty-two comedy duet scenes for teens.
  PS3601.L4324A28 2012
  808.8'017--dc23

                              2012023089

1 2 3   12 13 14

Table of Contents

Man and Woman 157

Two Women

1. Most Popular

CAST: ERICA, KAYLA
PROPS: Trophy, two ballots, pen, paper with list of names
SETTING: Auditorium

1   *(At rise, ERICA stands at the podium and speaks into a*
2   *microphone.)*
3 **ERICA: And the winner is ...**
4 **KAYLA:** *(Runs On-Stage.)* **I can't believe it!** *(Pushes ERICA*
5   *aside and grabs the trophy.)* **Thank you! Thank you!**
6   **Thank you all so much!**
7 **ERICA: Kayla, I didn't call out your name.**
8 **KAYLA:** *(Smiling, looking to the audience)* **Didn't you?**
9 **ERICA: No. I was about to announce the winner when you**
10   **ran up here and grabbed the award and thanked your**
11   **fellow students. A little premature, wouldn't you say?**
12 **KAYLA:** *(Smiling)* **I'm sorry. I was just so excited!** *(Steps*
13   *aside.)* **But you go ahead.** *(Hands the trophy back to her.)*
14   **Call out my name.**
15 **ERICA:** *(Glares at her, then speaks into the microphone.)* **And**
16   **the award this year for most popular girl is ...** *(Pauses,*
17   *looks at KAYLA, and then rolls her eyes)* **Kayla Stewart.**
18 **KAYLA:** *(Grabs the trophy and pushes ERICA aside.)* **I can't**
19   **believe it!**
20 **ERICA: You must have believed it since you were up here**
21   **before I even called your name.**
22 **KAYLA:** *(Into the microphone)* **Thank you! Thank you! Oh,**
23   **this means so much to me. I'm so touched. Now, I have**
24   **a few people I'd like to thank.** *(Pulls out a long list.)*
25 **ERICA: I see you came prepared.**
26 **KAYLA: First, I'd like to thank all my BFFs out there. Abigail,**
27   **Sonya, Madison, Ebony, Jasmine, Nicole —**
28 **ERICA: How many BFFs do you have?**

1   KAYLA: Twenty-eight. *(Looks back at her list.)* **There's Jade,**
2   **Jordan, Sydney, Destiny, Monique, Sara, Taylor, Amber** —
3   ERICA: Excuse me, but I thought you were only supposed
4   to have one BFF.
5   KAYLA: Not me.
6   ERICA: But that doesn't make sense. A BFF is your one and
7   only best friend forever. If you have more than one
8   BFF, then they're not your BFF. They're just your FF.
9   KAYLA: FF?
10 ERICA: Friend forever. That is until you get mad at them
11   or move away or start liking the same guy they like or
12   something like that.
13 KAYLA: Well, I have lots of BFFs. That's just the way it is.
14   *(Into the microphone)* **Next I'd like to thank all my**
15   **boyfriends. Matt, Kyle, Trevor, Jamal, Logan, Austin,**
16   **Gabriel** —
17 ERICA: So you have a lot of boyfriends like you have a lot
18   of girlfriends?
19 KAYLA: *(Smiles.)* **What can I say? I'm a popular girl! And to**
20   **all my exes ... guys, you know I still love you, but we**
21   **had to go our separate ways. Sid, Jameson, William,**
22   **David, Marshall, Zach, Billy, Kevin, Terrance** —
23 ERICA: Enough already with the ex-boyfriends. No one
24   cares about that.
25 KAYLA: And to all my other awesome friends out there,
26   you know I love each and every one of you. Logan,
27   Elizabeth, Tyler, Jasmine, Ashley, Brooke, Regan,
28   Blair, Alyssa —
29 ERICA: Are you going to name every single person in the
30   entire school?
31 KAYLA: Do I have time? *(Looking at her list)* **I still have a lot**
32   **of people I'd like to thank.**
33 ERICA: Thank them for what?
34 KAYLA: For their vote. For their friendship!
35 ERICA: Well ... you don't have to thank me.

1   KAYLA: Why not?

2   ERICA: Because I didn't vote for you.

3   KAYLA: What? You didn't vote for me?

4   ERICA: No. I voted for Bethany.

5   KAYLA: I can't believe it. Erica, how could you?

6   ERICA: In fact, I was on the Ballot Committee and it was a
7   very close call. There was only one vote between you
8   and Bethany. It wasn't a landslide like you thought.

9   KAYLA: You mean, I won by only one vote?

10 ERICA: That's right. It was almost a tie. You almost shared
11   your popular trophy here with Bethany Mitchell.

12 KAYLA: *(Crosses arms.)* I don't believe you.

13 ERICA: It's the truth. You came very close to losing.

14 KAYLA: *(Clutching her trophy. Into the microphone)* Thank
15   you so much for voting me as most popular! And to
16   all of you who I didn't get around to mentioning ...
17   *(Gives ERICA a glare)* I know you all agree that the
18   best ... well, the most popular girl won! And I can't tell
19   you what it feels like to be named most popular.

20 ERICA: Oh, wait! Wait! Wait just a minute here!

21 KAYLA: What?

22 ERICA: I just remembered.

23 KAYLA: What?

24 ERICA: I never voted. I was so busy counting the ballots
25   that I forgot to turn in my vote.

26 KAYLA: Oh well. Too late for you.

27 ERICA: No it's not. I have an extra ballot right here. *(Picks
28   up a pen and checks off a name on the ballot.)* There
29   you go. I voted.

30 KAYLA: *(Peering)* Who did you vote for?

31 ERICA: Bethany. Which means ...

32 KAYLA: Which means you missed the deadline. Votes are
33   in. Votes are counted and the decision has been
34   reached. *(Into the microphone)* Again, I want to thank
35   all my friends out there for voting for me. It just

1   means so much to me.

2   ERICA: Which means, it's a tie! *(Tries to push KAYLA aside.)*

3   Give me the mic.

4   KAYLA: No! *(Firmly holding onto the podium)*

5   ERICA: *(Pushing KAYLA)* Give it to me.

6   KAYLA: *(Into the microphone)* It's such an honor to be

7   named most popular. It's one of those things I look

8   forward to telling my children one day. "Yes, your

9   mother was the most popular girl in the entire

10   school. Want to see my trophy?"

11 ERICA: *(Pushes her aside. Into the microphone)* I'm sorry,

12   but there's been some confusion.

13 KAYLA: There is no confusion. I won! *(Smiles at audience.)*

14   Thank you! Thank you all so much!

15 ERICA: The contest was actually a tie.

16 KAYLA: No it wasn't. *(Smiles at audience.)* And no one is

17   more thankful to be voted most popular than me.

18 ERICA: *(Into the microphone)* And seeing that it was a tie,

19   we must call another girl to the stage to share in this

20   victory. And that would be Bethany Mitchell.

21   Bethany, would you please come to the stage?

22 KAYLA: Wait!

23 ERICA: For what?

24 KAYLA: You know what? I forgot to turn in my ballot.

25 ERICA: Seriously?

26 KAYLA: Seriously! I was so busy preparing my acceptance

27   speech that I forgot to turn in my ballot. *(Reaches into*

28   *her pocket and takes out a ballot.)* And if your ballot is

29   accepted late, then so is mine. *(Hands her the ballot.)*

30   Here! *(Smiles.)* And of course I voted for myself.

31 ERICA: *(Looks at the ballot. Into the microphone)* And the

32   winner this year for most popular girl is ...

33 KAYLA: *(Pushes ERICA aside and speaks into the*

34   *microphone.)* Me! I don't know what to say. I can't

35   believe it! Thank you. Oh, thank you all so much!

2. Free

CAST: BROOKE, CARRIE
PROPS: Box with the word "Free" written on the outside, odd-looking hat
SETTING: Street corner

1   *(At rise, CARRIE stands on a street corner holding a box.*
2   *BROOKE enters, stops, and looks at CARRIE.)*
3   **BROOKE: Free?**
4   **CARRIE:** *(Holds out the box.)* **It's all yours.**
5   **BROOKE: Let me guess. A kitten. No, thank you. You**
6   **couldn't pay me to take one of those horrid animals**
7   **that will claw my furniture to pieces, shed on**
8   **everything, demand I pet it when it so chooses, jump**
9   **on my counters, and give me the worst allergies I've**
10   **ever experienced. So no. No, thank you.**
11   **CARRIE: It's not a kitten.**
12   **BROOKE: And I don't want a puppy either.**
13   **CARRIE: It's not a puppy.**
14   **BROOKE: Then what? What are you giving away for free?**
15   **CARRIE:** *(Holds out the box.)* **Don't you want it?**
16   **BROOKE: What I want is to know what's inside the box.**
17   **CARRIE: If it could be anything you wanted, what would it**
18   **be?**
19   **BROOKE: Uh ... a million dollars.**
20   **CARRIE: But money doesn't make you happy.**
21   **BROOKE: I disagree. Give me a million dollars and see how**
22   **happy I am.**
23   **CARRIE: It'd only be temporary.**
24   **BROOKE: If you've got a million dollars in that box, I'll take**
25   **it. If not, like I said, I'm allergic to cats, and I don't want**
26   **anything that I have to take care of.**
27   **CARRIE: It's not a million dollars.**

1   **BROOKE:** Of course not. But I bet it sounds like this.
2   "Meow. Meow."
3   **CARRIE:** I told you it wasn't a kitten.
4   **BROOKE:** Then what's in the box?
5   **CARRIE:** And it's not a million dollars.
6   **BROOKE:** Is it a secret?
7   **CARRIE:** Only until you accept it.
8   **BROOKE:** So you're saying that I don't get to find out
9   what's inside the box until I take it?
10 **CARRIE:** Yes. *(Holds out the box.)* And it's free! Here.
11 **BROOKE:** Why are you doing this?
12 **CARRIE:** Just trying to make someone's day.
13 **BROOKE:** Are you like the Secret Santa who hands out
14   free gifts to people?
15 **CARRIE:** I can see the similarities.
16 **BROOKE:** So you're doing this out of the goodness of your
17   heart?
18 **CARRIE:** Yes I am.
19 **BROOKE:** Do you have any more boxes? Can I choose from
20   a selection?
21 **CARRIE:** This is the one and only. *(Holds out the box.)* And
22   it's yours for the taking. It's your lucky day.
23 **BROOKE:** My lucky day, huh?
24 **CARRIE:** Yes. Here you go!
25 **BROOKE:** No, thank you.
26 **CARRIE:** You don't want it?
27 **BROOKE:** No, because I don't know what's in it.
28 **CARRIE:** But it's free.
29 **BROOKE:** Free or not, that doesn't mean it's a good thing.
30 **CARRIE:** But it is. I promise.
31 **BROOKE:** Then let me see what's inside the box. Then I'll
32   decide if I want it or not.
33 **CARRIE:** Then that'll ruin the surprise.
34 **BROOKE:** The surprise? It's not like you're giving me a
35   Christmas present. So open it up and let me see

1   what's inside.

2   CARRIE: *(Holds out the box.)* **Take it and you can see**

3   **what's inside.**

4   **BROOKE: And when I take it, I'm stuck with it. Right?**

5   **CARRIE: Yes.** Then it will be all yours.

6   **BROOKE: And it'll do this, "Meow, meow, meow."** And

7   **then you'll run off and I'll be sneezing my head off.**

8   **And crying. And yelling for you to come back. But it**

9   **will be too late.**

10 **CARRIE: I told you it's not a kitten.**

11 **BROOKE: Question. Is it alive?**

12 **CARRIE: No it's not.**

13 **BROOKE: Well, that's good. And you're giving it away**

14   **because ... ?**

15 **CARRIE: Because I want to.**

16 **BROOKE: Because I want to?! What kind of answer is that?**

17 **CARRIE: Do you want it or not? Last chance.**

18 **BROOKE: Last chance?**

19 **CARRIE: If you don't want it, someone else will. Hey,**

20   **maybe that person over there would like it. I'll go see.**

21   *(Starts to leave.)*

22 **BROOKE: Hold on! Just hold on!**

23 **CARRIE: So you want it?**

24 **BROOKE: Just give it to me.**

25 **CARRIE: OK.** *(Hands her the box.)* **Hope you enjoy it.**

26 *(Exits.)*

27 **BROOKE: What is this?** *(Opens the box and pulls out an*

28   *odd-looking hat. She stares at it for a moment, and then*

29   *puts it on. Looking ahead, she smiles proudly.)* **I like it.**

30 *(As she exits.)* **And it was free!**

3. Counseling Session

CAST: MRS. KIMBLE, VICTORIA
PROPS: Tissues
SETTING: Counselor's office

1   *(At rise, VICTORIA enters the office.)*
2   **MRS. KIMBLE: May I help you?**
3   **VICTORIA: Are you the counselor?**
4   **MRS. KIMBLE: I am. I'm Mrs. Kimble.**
5   **VICTORIA: Do you have time to see me? I hope so, because I**
6   **have major problems. You know, I bet you get sick of**
7   **hearing about problems, don't you? Is any of it**
8   **exciting? Do you always swear to confidentiality?**
9   **Because I can't have you blabbing my problems to the**
10   **whole school. You don't do that, do you? Did you say**
11   **you have time to see me?**
12   **MRS. KIMBLE: Sit down.**
13   **VICTORIA: Oh good. Because I have got to talk to someone.**
14   **And who better than the school counselor? But you**
15   **swear what is spoken here stays here? Kind of like what**
16   **happens in Vegas stays in Vegas. Not that I've ever been**
17   **to Vegas. But you know what I mean. You know, you**
18   **should get a sign for your door that says, "What**
19   **happens in here, stays in here." But anyway, so you**
20   **have time for a little counseling session here?**
21   **MRS. KIMBLE: Why don't you catch your breath.**
22   **VICTORIA:** *(Takes a deep breath.)* **Yes, I needed to do that.**
23   *(Takes another deep breath.)* **Really needed that!** *(Looks*
24   *around the room.)* **Wow. I can't believe I'm really in**
25   **here. I didn't think I'd have the guts to step into your**
26   **office. You know, it's like once you step in here, you're**
27   **admitting you have a problem. Oh, gosh. That's what**
28   **I've done, haven't I? Admitted I have a problem. Which**

1   you swear on your life that you won't blab to the
2   whole school or the other teachers?
3   MRS. KIMBLE: I don't blab.
4   VICTORIA: Of course you don't. If you did you wouldn't be
5   able to keep your job. And I bet it's a depressing job
6   listening to problems all day long. "My boyfriend
7   broke my heart." "I'm failing school." "I hate my
8   mom." "I hate my dad." "Someone is bullying me."
9   Does it ever make you want to talk to someone
10   yourself?
11   MRS. KIMBLE: Excuse me?
12   VICTORIA: Like go to counseling yourself after
13   counseling students all day. Because I'm telling you,
14   it would me. You know, I think it'd make me go a
15   little nuts-oh.
16   MRS. KIMBLE: Are you going to let me say anything here?
17   VICTORIA: Of course! I'm sorry! I'm rattling on, aren't I?
18   I didn't mean to. I guess I'm nervous. I mean, who
19   wants to admit they have a problem. *(Raises hand.)*
20   Not me! But who has a problem? *(Raises hand.)* Me!
21   That was hard to admit, you know? Whew! I already
22   feel better by just admitting I have a problem. Hello,
23   my name is Victoria, and I have a problem.
24   MRS. KIMBLE: Let's talk about your problem.
25   VICTORIA: Oh no. Here comes the hard part.
26   MRS. KIMBLE: Family problems?
27   VICTORIA: Oh, no! My family is fine. I mean, except for
28   the occasional argument with my mom. For example,
29   last night, she wanted me to help Timmy with his
30   stupid spelling words. And I'm like, why should I
31   have to do that? I've got friends to call, status updates
32   to enter, messages to text, emails to read, music to
33   listen to. I don't have time to call out fourth grade
34   spelling words. So the word is meat and he spells it
35   m-e-e-t. I'm like, "No, Timmy, it's the kind of meat

1   you eat, not when you meet someone for lunch." But

2   he didn't get it so we had to go over it again and again

3   and again. Seriously? How hard is it to differentiate

4   between the meat you eat and when you go to meet

5   someone? Obviously it was for a fourth grader! I hope

6   he made a hundred on his spelling test after I

7   sacrificed my social life to help him study.

8 MRS. KIMBLE: Back to your problem.

9 VICTORIA: Oh, my problem. Yes, back to that. Like we all

10   want to hear about that! But that is why I came in

11   here. To talk about *my problem.*

12 MRS. KIMBLE: And your problem is ... ?

13 VICTORIA: Do you have any tissues? Because I feel like I

14   might cry. *(Looks around the room.)* Surely a

15   counselor's office has tissues.

16 MRS. KIMBLE: *(Hands her a box of tissues.)* Here.

17 VICTORIA: Thank you. *(Pulls out a tissue.)* I bet you go

18   through a ton of these, don't you?

19 MRS. KIMBLE: So why don't you tell me —

20 VICTORIA: Hold on! Let me take another one of those

21   deep breaths. I think it helps. *(Breathes deeply.)* I hope

22   I don't cry. Is it OK if I walk around the room while I

23   talk? Somehow it makes me feel better. *(Stands and*

24   *walks around.)* I think this will help. Sort of clears my

25   head. Helps me gather my thoughts. *(Grabs the box of*

26   *tissues.)* Oh, I think I'll hold on to these while I move

27   about the room. Just in case. Oh, where do I start?

28   Where do I start?

29 MRS. KIMBLE: How about you start by telling me what

30   your problem is?

31 VICTORIA: The problem is, I don't know what to do.

32   Option A or Option B? Or I guess I could do nothing

33   and let the chips fall where they may. But what would

34   you do?

35 MRS. KIMBLE: I'd have to hear what your problem is first.

1 VICTORIA: But say you had a problem ...
2 MRS. KIMBLE: I'm starting to think I have one right now.
3 VICTORIA: Do you go with your gut feeling, which is
4   Option A, or do you go with the safe, practical
5   decision, which is Option B? Or do nothing and just
6   let fate take care of it?
7 MRS. KIMBLE: It depends on what the problem is.
8 VICTORIA: But tell me, do you lean toward your instincts
9   or toward being safe and practical? Or just shrug it
10   off?
11 MRS. KIMBLE: I like to weigh all my options.
12 VICTORIA: Which is what I'm doing!
13 MRS. KIMBLE: And all being equal, I go with my gut
14   feeling.
15 VICTORIA: Of course! Go with your gut feeling. That's
16   what I've wanted to do all along, but I guess I just
17   needed someone to tell me that was the right thing to
18   do. And that's what I'm going to do. Go with my gut
19   feeling. Wow. I feel so much better. I don't even feel
20   like crying now. *(Hands the box of tissues to MRS.*
21   *KIMBLE.)* **Wait!** *(Pulls one tissue from the box.)* **I** might
22   need one tissue when I tell Coach Phillips that it was
23   Miss Richard's fault that the school's Spirit and Pride
24   T-shirts were ordered with the word *spirit*
25   misspelled because she was too busy flirting with Mr.
26   Hollister across the hall when I asked her if the
27   layout looked OK before I took it to the printer and
28   she nodded and said, "Go, go." So I went and now the
29   school has to pay for one thousand, two hundred T-
30   shirts for all the students to wear at the playoffs that
31   say "Wildcats Sprite and Pride," which no one will
32   want to wear since it says sprite instead of spirit.
33   *Sprite and pride?* That doesn't sound too good, does
34   it? I didn't know spirit had two *i's* in it. Did you?
35   Oops. And what's funny is that I was the one helping

1   Timmy with his spelling words. How ironic is that?
2   Well, anyway, Coach Phillips will start yelling at Miss
3   Richards and probably at me, too. Then Mr. Hollister
4   will probably rush out in the hall and yell at Coach
5   Phillips for making Miss Richards cry and then I
6   might start crying too. I hope they don't get into a fist
7   fight. But yes, I think going with my gut feeling is the
8   best. Thank you! *(Exits.)*
9 MRS. KIMBLE: *(Jumps up.)* Wait! Wait! Come back! Let's
10   talk about this!

4. A New Me

CAST: ANNA, ERIN
SETTING: School hallway

1   **ANNA:** *(Pointing)* **Your hair!**
2   **ERIN: Don't you love it?**
3   **ANNA: But it's blonde.** *(Or say another color, opposite of what*
4   *the actor has.)*
5   **ERIN: I know! I colored it last night. Don't you love it?**
6   **ANNA: But it's blonde.** *(Or say another color.)*
7   **ERIN: I know! Isn't it crazy? All my life I've had dark** *(Or say*
8   *light)* **hair and look at me now. Don't you just love it?**
9   **ANNA: I think so.**
10 **ERIN: You think so? You have to love it. It's so me.**
11 **ANNA: But I'm not used to seeing you like this. It's crazy. Are**
12   **my eyes deceiving me? Now you're ... you're ...**
13 **ERIN: Blonde!** *(Or say another color.)*
14 **ANNA: Don't get me wrong, I like it. It's just going to take me**
15   **awhile to get used it. It's like you're a different person.**
16 **ERIN: I know! Who would've thought that a little hair color**
17   **could change your entire life?**
18 **ANNA: Well, it has. I mean ... wow. I don't know what to say.**
19   **It's cute, it's crazy ... it's like I'm seeing you, but my eyes**
20   **are playing tricks on me.**
21 **ERIN: Everyone I've run into today has loved it. And they tell**
22   **me this is the color I should've been born with.**
23 **ANNA: I never even thought of you as a blonde.** *(Or say*
24   *another color.)*
25 **ERIN: Me neither. But yesterday I woke up, looked in the**
26   **mirror, and thought, you know, I'd look good with**
27   **blonde hair.** *(Flips hair.)* **And I do!**
28 **ANNA: Yes, you do. But what an abrupt change. I still feel**
29   **like my eyes are playing tricks on me.**

1   ERIN: You know, it's getting to be a fairly standard thing to
2   do. Natalie dyed her hair red and Isabel went jet
3   black. Oh, and Vicky put black streaks in her blonde
4   hair. And a couple of weeks ago I saw a girl in the mall
5   with purple hair. Let me tell you, it looked amazing.
6   ANNA: I'd love to do something like that, but my mother
7   wouldn't let me.
8   ERIN: Neither would mine.
9   ANNA: Uh-oh. Has she seen you yet?
10 ERIN: This morning when I walked into the kitchen.
11 ANNA: Oh no! What did she say?
12 ERIN: Nothing.
13 ANNA: Nothing?
14 ERIN: Well, nothing at first. Then she screamed. Then she
15   was like this. *(Grabs her hair and demonstrates.)* "Tell
16   me that is a wig! Tell me that is a wig right now, or ...
17   or ... Because if it's not, I'm going to ... !" Then she
18   pulled my hair then screamed. I was like, "Ouch,
19   Mom! That hurt!" Then she screamed again.
20 ANNA: Wow.
21 ERIN: Yeah, it wasn't a pretty sight.
22 ANNA: Are you in trouble?
23 ERIN: I don't know. When she started screaming again, I
24   grabbed my backpack and ran out the door. I guess
25   I'll find out when I get home. But hopefully Mom will
26   calm down by the time I get home from school.
27   Besides, what's done is done. I'm now a blonde. So
28   what can she do about it at this point?
29 ANNA: Kill you.
30 ERIN: Oh, she might make me wash the dishes after
31   dinner tonight or maybe for the entire week, but
32   Mom's a softy. And I think by the time dinner is over
33   with, she'll get used to the new me.
34 ANNA: You know, come to think of it, I'd like a new me,
35   too.

1 ERIN: You should color your hair, too! Then everyone you
2   run into will give you all this attention and tell you
3   how awesome you look. A few of my friends have said
4   this color makes me look smart. Do you think so? Do
5   I look smart?
6 ANNA: You do. But I don't really care about looking smart.
7   I'd rather look desirable. And maybe then Joey
8   McPherson would notice me.
9 ERIN: Then go blonde. *(Or say another color opposite of the*
10   *actress.)*
11 ANNA: You really think I should?
12 ERIN: Yes! And I could help you color your hair tonight if
13   you'd like.
14 ANNA: You mean if you're not grounded.
15 ERIN: Mom never really grounds me. And even if she
16   does, I just give her my pitiful look. Like this.
17   *(Demonstrates.)* And then I'm off the hook. Yes, I have
18   my mom wrapped around my little finger.
19 ANNA: Then let's do it! I think I want to dye my hair red
20   and purple.
21 ERIN: Yes! Red and purple! We'll do streaks!
22 ANNA: Do you think it'll look good on me?
23 ERIN: I think it'll look awesome!
24 ANNA: Good, because I like the idea of a new me. A little
25   red and purple hair and my life might turn explosive.
26 ERIN: Explosive, huh? Like a firecracker?
27 ANNA: That's what I'm hoping for.
28 ERIN: Then we'll do it tonight. And tomorrow morning
29   you can come to school with red and purple
30   dynamite hair.
31 ANNA: Dynamite hair! I like that.
32 ERIN: *(As they exit)* It's going to look so cute.
33 ANNA: I'm so excited. I can't wait. And look out Joey
34   McPherson!

5. Text Rumors

CAST: SIERRA, TONYA
PROPS: Two cell phones
SETTING: School hallway

1   **SIERRA: I hate my life.**
2   **TONYA: Again?**
3   **SIERRA: Everyone hates me.**
4   **TONYA: I don't.**
5   **SIERRA: Hailey said Blake was going to break up with me by**
6   **noon.**
7   **TONYA: How would she know?**
8   **SIERRA: Text rumor.**
9   **TONYA: And? Did it happen?**
10 **SIERRA: Yes. At eleven forty-three a.m. Blake told me it was**
11   **over.**
12 **TONYA: In person?**
13 **SIERRA: Of course not. Who breaks up in person? He passed**
14   **me a note in algebra and said he liked me as a friend,**
15   **but he was breaking up.**
16 **TONYA: Why didn't he text you?**
17 **SIERRA: Because he's grounded. His parents took his phone**
18   **away.**
19 **TONYA: Bummer.**
20 **SIERRA: Bummer that his parents took his phone away or**
21   **that he broke up with me?**
22 **TONYA: Both.**
23 **SIERRA: Yeah, he broke up with me by a stinking note! You**
24   **know, that's how kids used to communicate in the**
25   **olden days. Notes. Can you even imagine? How did they**
26   **survive without texting?**
27 **TONYA: I don't know. I couldn't. Well, I say, so what if Blake**
28   **dumped you.**

1   SIERRA: So what?

2   TONYA: There are plenty more fish in the sea.

3   SIERRA: Who says that? Plenty more fish in the sea?

4   TONYA: That's what my mom told me when Justin broke

5   my heart. "Honey, don't you worry. He isn't worth a

6   second thought. And take this from someone who

7   knows. There are plenty more fish in the sea." And

8   it's true. I'm happier with Chris than I ever was with

9   Justin.

10 SIERRA: Well, I'm over Blake.

11 TONYA: Great! Then you can stop hating your life now.

12 SIERRA: No I can't because in fifth period I realized I was

13   in love with Michael. He sits three chairs in front of

14   me. And guess what?

15 TONYA: What?

16 SIERRA: He hates my guts.

17 TONYA: How do you know he hates your guts?

18 SIERRA: Because in fifth period, I told Jennifer I was in

19   love with Michael and within five minutes he was

20   turning around in his chair giving me dirty looks.

21 TONYA: I don't understand. How could he know?

22 SIERRA: Text rumors! They get around so fast. Too fast!

23 TONYA: But you don't know what someone else told him.

24   And how could Michael believe every text he reads?

25   Most rumors aren't true.

26 SIERRA: Oh, Michael got the right message all right. In

27   sixth period, his best friend, Charlie, texted me and

28   told me to give it up because Michael wasn't

29   interested.

30 TONYA: Wow.

31 SIERRA: And by the time sixth period was over, half the

32   school was either telling me not to chase after

33   someone who didn't share my feelings or giving me

34   sympathy for getting my heart broken.

35 TONYA: I didn't hear about it. Well, at least not yet. But I

1   do have my phone on silent and I haven't checked it

2   for a while. *(Looks at her phone. Reads aloud.)* **Sierra**

3   **told Michael she loves him and guess what?** *(Looks at*

4   *SIERRA.)* **Text rumors sure do get around, don't they?**

5   SIERRA: Read the rest of the message.

6   TONYA: Uh, OK. *(Looks at phone.)* **And guess what?**

7   SIERRA: What?

8   TONYA: *Michael thinks she's awesome but he has a*

9   *girlfriend. (Looks at SIERRA.)* Well, that was nice.

10   SIERRA: That's not what it says. Tell me the truth!

11   TONYA: You are a great person.

12   SIERRA: I'm pathetic! Oh, I hate my life.

13   TONYA: Sierra, remember what I said.

14   SIERRA: What?

15   TONYA: There are plenty more fish in the sea.

16   SIERRA: But I don't want a fish!

17   TONYA: What about Brandon?

18   SIERRA: What about Brandon?

19   TONYA: Well, you said you loved him last Friday.

20   Remember?

21   SIERRA: I don't love Brandon anymore. After I saw his

22   impression of a hyena in the library last week, I was

23   over him.

24   TONYA: Brandon was imitating a hyena?

25   SIERRA: That's what it looked like to me.

26   TONYA: So since Blake broke up with you and Michael's

27   not interested and you're over Brandon, who do you

28   like?

29   SIERRA: No one! I hate boys. Period. And did I mention

30   that I hate my life?

31   TONYA: Yes, you did mention that. But surely there's one

32   boy out there ... one fish in the sea ...

33   SIERRA: I hate fish.

34   TONYA: Chris?

35   SIERRA: No.

1 TONYA: Zach?

2 SIERRA: No.

3 TONYA: Seth?

4 SIERRA: Who?

5 TONYA: Seth who drives the silver Mustang.

6 SIERRA: Well, he is cute.

7 TONYA: I like his car.

8 SIERRA: So do I.

9 TONYA: And I heard he and Sydney broke up.

10 SIERRA: They did?

11 TONYA: Which means ...

12 SIERRA: He's available! *(Smiling)* Well, in that case ...

13 TONYA: You could text him.

14 SIERRA: I don't know. Maybe you could text him for me.

15 TONYA: And say what?

16 SIERRA: Tell him you heard something interesting.

17 TONYA: Like what?

18 SIERRA: That I like him. Then see what he says.

19 TONYA: OK. *(Sends a text message.)* **Hey, Seth, I heard**

20   **Sierra likes you.**

21 SIERRA: What did he say?

22 TONYA: Nothing yet.

23 SIERRA: What do you think he'll say?

24 TONYA: I don't have a clue.

25 SIERRA: Do you think he likes me?

26 TONYA: I think there's a good chance. Oh, he sent me a

27   text back. *(Looks at her phone.)*

28 SIERRA: What? What did he say?

29 TONYA: Oh ...

30 SIERRA: What? What? Tell me?

31 TONYA: He said he likes you as a friend.

32 SIERRA: *Oh!* I hate my life!

33 TONYA: No you don't.

34 SIERRA: Yes I do.

35 TONYA: There are other guys out there.

1   **SIERRA: I know! Other fish in the sea. And didn't I tell you**
2   **that I hate fish? I hate them with a passion!**
3   **TONYA: Oh look!**
4   **SIERRA: What?**
5   **TONYA: It's a text rumor.**
6   **SIERRA: What? The whole world only likes me as their**
7   **friend?**
8   **TONYA: Phil. He likes you big time.**
9   **SIERRA: He does?**
10   **TONYA: Should I text him and tell him to go jump in the**
11   **lake? You know, fish should be in the lake and since**
12   **you hate them —**
13   **SIERRA: No! No! Tell him I like him, too.**
14   **TONYA: You do?**
15   **SIERRA: I do!**
16   **TONYA:** *(Texting)* **Oh, brother.**
17   **SIERRA: Yes, I like Phil! And I could see the two of us**
18   **together. Yes, me and Phil. A perfect pair. In fact, I**
19   **think I'm falling in love with him right now.**
20   **TONYA:** *(After she finishes sending a text)* **It's set.**
21   **SIERRA: What?**
22   **TONYA: You and Phil are hooked up. Boyfriend and**
23   **girlfriend.**
24   **SIERRA: Already?**
25   **TONYA: Already. Isn't modern technology amazing? I'd**
26   **hate to live in the olden days when they had to pass**
27   **notes.**
28   **SIERRA: I know! Me, too.**

6. Evil Twin

CAST: LAUREN, TAYLOR
SETTING: Bedroom

1 LAUREN: We may share birthdays, parents, a bedroom, and
2   live in the same house, but I refuse to acknowledge you
3   as my twin sister in high school this year.
4 TAYLOR: Lauren, why are you being so mean?
5 LAUREN: Because I want to be known as me, not Taylor's
6   twin sister. And now that we've moved to a new town
7   and new school with new friends, let's keep the fact
8   that we're related to ourselves. I don't know you and
9   you don't know me. Got it?
10 TAYLOR: If that's what you want.
11 LAUREN: It is.
12 TAYLOR: And since we don't look anything alike, who'd ever
13   know the truth? But the truth is you and I are twin
14   sisters.
15 LAUREN: Taylor, never mention that again. I don't know
16   you and you don't know me.
17 TAYLOR: But you know, Lauren, people may become
18   suspicious when our mother drops us off at school and
19   picks us up in the afternoon. Plus the fact that we do
20   share the same last name. That you can't lie about.
21 LAUREN: OK, if we have to admit to anything, we're sisters.
22   But let's see if we can avoid that subject, OK?
23 TAYLOR: Can I be the older sister?
24 LAUREN: Sure.
25 TAYLOR: But wait. If we're in the same grade at school it'll
26   look like I failed a year seeing that I'm the older sister
27   and I'm in the same grade as my younger sister.
28 LAUREN: Then you be the younger sister. I'll be the older,
29   dumber sister. That is, if we have to admit to being

1   related.

2   TAYLOR: Or we could say we were homeschooled until

3   this year and we are equally smart. That sounds good.

4   LAUREN: Whatever. As long as we're not twins. Because

5   I'm so sick of hearing, "Oh, you're Taylor's twin sister.

6   It's just so hard to understand how *that* happened."

7   TAYLOR: That's because I'm the nice twin and you're the

8   ... well ... you know.

9   LAUREN: What? Say it!

10   TAYLOR: Well, Mom always did say you were a little devil.

11   LAUREN: Oh, so I'm the evil twin now?

12   TAYLOR: Oh, Lauren, you know that I love you.

13   LAUREN: Keep that love stuff out of this. You and I both

14   know we're as opposite as they come.

15   TAYLOR: Well, that's true. I love life. Love people. Love

16   children. Love animals. In fact, I love everyone!

17   LAUREN: And I'm usually angry at the world. Don't like

18   many people. Including you. And I'm not an animal

19   lover.

20   TAYLOR: And I love shopping, fashion –

21   LAUREN: Hate shopping. Hate the mall. Give me a pair of

22   jeans and a T-shirt and I'm good.

23   TAYLOR: And I love school. Honor Roll student, here!

24   LAUREN: Hate school. Especially when I hear, "Oh, you're

25   Taylor's twin sister!" Then they look at me and shake

26   their head and wonder what happened.

27   TAYLOR: Oh, Lauren, you're exaggerating. Everyone loves

28   you.

29   LAUREN: And I just want to pluck their eyes out.

30   TAYLOR: Lauren, why are you being so mean?

31   LAUREN: Because I feel mean inside.

32   TAYLOR: Well, you need to feel the love.

33   LAUREN: Well, I don't.

34   TAYLOR: I wonder why?

35   LAUREN: Maybe because you hogged all the space in

1   Mom's belly before we were born and it made me
2   mad.
3   TAYLOR: What? You're blaming me for taking up more
4   than my fair share in Mom's belly?
5   LAUREN: Yes! And you elbowed me like a millions times.
6   TAYLOR: You couldn't remember that.
7   LAUREN: Well, I do. And after nine months of being hit by
8   you, I'd had it.
9   TAYLOR: I'm sorry, but I don't remember hitting you in
10   Mom's belly. And if I did, I'm sure it was an accident.
11   I would never hit my twin sister on purpose and you
12   know that. I love you, Lauren.
13   LAUREN: Then you come out all cute and sweet and
14   cuddly. And I come out fussy and angry at the world.
15   Mom did say I was a terrible baby. And you know
16   whose fault it was? Yours!
17   TAYLOR: Me? For elbowing you in Mom's tummy?
18   LAUREN: Yes. It's your fault, Taylor.
19   TAYLOR: But how could I have known what I was doing?
20   LAUREN: I don't know. But now you do!
21   TAYLOR: Then tell me, how can I fix this? How can I make
22   it right?
23   LAUREN: By admitting that my crummy disposition is all
24   *your* fault.
25   TAYLOR: My fault? Seriously?
26   LAUREN: Yes.
27   TAYLOR: Well, I don't know what to do except apologize.
28   Lauren, I'm sorry for being a hog in Mom's tummy.
29   And I'm sorry for elbowing you like a gazillion times.
30   LAUREN: And kicking me.
31   TAYLOR: And kicking you. If I could take it all back, I would.
32   Lauren, you're my favorite sister in the entire world.
33   LAUREN: I'm your only sister.
34   TAYLOR: You're my favorite only sister. *(Hugs her.)* I love
35   you!

1   **LAUREN:** *(Pushes her away.)* **Stop! Stop it with that love**
2   **stuff.**
3   **TAYLOR: But I love you.** *(Elbows her as she tries to hug her*
4   *again.)*
5   **LAUREN: See! There you go. You just hit me with your**
6   **elbow.**
7   **TAYLOR: I'm sorry! I was just trying to give you a hug.**
8   **LAUREN: Is that what you were trying to do in Mom's**
9   **belly?**
10   **TAYLOR: I'm sure it was. I love you, Lauren! Do you**
11   **forgive me?**
12   **LAUREN: I don't know. I guess.**
13   **TAYLOR: So now can we tell everyone at school that we're**
14   **twin sisters?**
15   **LAUREN: I don't think so.**
16   **TAYLOR: You know, Lauren, we'll probably have**
17   **homeroom together. We always do. Sisters. Best**
18   **friends forever!**
19   **LAUREN: Drop the best friends forever. I can barely**
20   **tolerate you.**
21   **TAYLOR: And we could dress the same every day. Like**
22   **Mom used to dress us alike when we were small.**
23   **Wouldn't that be fun?**
24   **LAUREN: No!**
25   **TAYLOR: And have lunch together.**
26   **LAUREN: No!**
27   **TAYLOR: And try out for cheerleader together!**
28   **LAUREN: No way!**
29   **TAYLOR:** *(Cheering)* **Go, team, go! Go, team, go!**
30   **LAUREN: No, Taylor. Let's go back to my original plan.**
31   **TAYLOR:** *(Disappointed)* **We aren't twins?**
32   **LAUREN: That's right. You don't know me and I don't**
33   **know you.**
34   **TAYLOR: If that's what you want.**
35   **LAUREN: It is.**

1   **TAYLOR: But Lauren ...**
2   **LAUREN: What?!**
3   **TAYLOR:** *(Throws her arms around her.)* **I love you!**
4   **LAUREN: Yuck. Stop it! Get away. Stop!**

7. Cry Me a River

CAST: NAIDA, EMMA
SETTING: School hallway
PROPS: Tissues

1 NAIDA: Emma, what's wrong?
2 EMMA: *(Dabbing her eyes with a tissue)* **Mr. Short**
3 **embarrassed me in class.**
4 NAIDA: What happened?
5 EMMA: I forgot to bring my art project to school.
6 NAIDA: Bring it tomorrow.
7 EMMA: It was due today. Everyone else brought their
8 projects, but not me.
9 NAIDA: It happens.
10 EMMA: Well, Mr. Short decided to use my forgetfulness as
11 an example to the entire class.
12 NAIDA: Uh-oh.
13 EMMA: Mr. Short said I had to stand in front of the class and
14 explain why I left my project at home.
15 NAIDA: That's stupid.
16 EMMA: I know. And you know me. I can't stand being put on
17 the spot. "Hey, everyone, look at me!" I don't like that
18 kind of thing.
19 NAIDA: I know! I remember last year when Mrs. Miller
20 asked you to stand and read your essay aloud.
21 EMMA: I was like, "I ... I ... I ... I ... " I couldn't make the words
22 come out.
23 NAIDA: Frozen like a Popsicle. So what happened when Mr.
24 Short made you stand in front of the class today?
25 EMMA: I cried.
26 NAIDA: Oh, no! Emma, I'm so sorry!
27 EMMA: I was like this. *(Demonstrates as she cries.)*
28 NAIDA: Oh, Emma. What did Mr. Short say when you were

1   crying?
2   EMMA: He said, "Oh, cry me a river!"
3   NAIDA: He said what?
4   EMMA: He said, "Oh, cry me a river!"
5   NAIDA: Cry me a river?
6   EMMA: I think I left a river of tears between all the desks
7   in his room.
8   NAIDA: He didn't feel sorry for you and let you sit down?
9   EMMA: No! He said, "The class is still waiting for you to
10   explain why your project was left at home and not
11   brought to class." And I was doing this. *(Cries.)* And
12   he said crying wouldn't get me out of it.
13   NAIDA: How mean!
14   EMMA: Then I finally managed to get a few words out
15   between the sobs. *(Demonstrates.)* "The reason ... the
16   reason ... I left ... my project ... is ... is ... is ... "
17   NAIDA: Oh, you poor thing!
18   EMMA: *(Still demonstrating)* "Is because ... is because ... I
19   set it down next to the Lucky Charms ... "
20   NAIDA: Lucky Charms?
21   EMMA: My cereal.
22   NAIDA: Oh.
23   EMMA: *(Continues demonstration.)* "And I was eating
24   breakfast ... and ... then realized I was going to be late.
25   So I grabbed my backpack ... coat, and keys and ran
26   out the door. When I got to school ... I looked down ...
27   and ... and ... said, 'Oh, no.'"
28   NAIDA: You forgot your art project.
29   EMMA: Instead of grabbing my art project, I grabbed the
30   Lucky Charms.
31   NAIDA: Oh, how funny! *(Looks at EMMA.)* Well, not that
32   funny. I mean kinda, but not really funny. I mean, if
33   you hadn't gotten into trouble and been embarrassed
34   in front of the entire class, it would've been funny.
35   EMMA: And then everyone started laughing at me. So I

1   started crying even louder.

2 NAIDA: What did Mr. Short say?

3 EMMA: "Oh, cry me a river!"

4 NAIDA: He must like saying that.

5 EMMA: Then he said prove it.

6 NAIDA: Prove what?

7 EMMA: He ordered me to go to my car and bring in the box

8   of Lucky Charms cereal to prove the story I was

9   telling.

10 NAIDA: He thought you were lying?

11 EMMA: Yes! So I ran to my car then came back inside the

12   room and handed him my box of Lucky Charms.

13 NAIDA: What did he say then?

14 EMMA: He said, "Oh ... and I thought you were lying."

15 NAIDA: What did you say?

16 EMMA: Nothing. I just stood in front of the classroom

17   clutching my box of Lucky Charms. Like this. *(Cries.)*

18 NAIDA: You were still crying?

19 EMMA: Yes! He embarrassed me.

20 NAIDA: I bet you'll never do that again.

21 EMMA: That's what Mr. Short said. He said he bet I'd never

22   bring Lucky Charms to school again instead of my art

23   project. And then he asked if he could have some.

24 NAIDA: Some what?

25 EMMA: Some of my Lucky Charms.

26 NAIDA: Mr. Short wanted to eat your cereal?

27 EMMA: Yes!

28 NAIDA: What did you do?

29 EMMA: I gave him my Lucky Charms and he stuck his

30   hand in the box and started eating them. One

31   handful after another.

32 NAIDA: How rude!

33 EMMA: I know. And he ate all of it, too.

34 NAIDA: What did you do?

35 EMMA: I cried.

1   **NAIDA: Again?**

2   **EMMA: Yes! That's my favorite cereal and Mr. Short ate it**

3   **all.**

4   **NAIDA: How mean! That's like stealing. You should tell**

5   **someone in the office.**

6   **EMMA: I did. After class I ran to Mrs. Baker and told her**

7   **what Mr. Short did. I was still in tears and I was like,**

8   **"Mrs. Baker, Mr. Short ate all my Lucky Charms!"**

9   *(Cries.)* **It's my favorite cereal and my mom won't buy**

10   **me any more until next week and ... and you know**

11   **what Mrs. Baker said?**

12 **NAIDA:** *(Shaking her head)* **No, what?**

13 **EMMA: "Oh, cry me a river!"**

14 **NAIDA: She didn't?**

15 **EMMA: She did. So now not only did Mr. Short humiliate**

16   **me and inhale all my Lucky Charms, no one in the**

17   **school even cares!**

18 **NAIDA: I care, Emma. But you've got to stop crying. Come**

19   **on. Stop crying. Emma ... You are going to cry a river,**

20   **aren't you?** *(EMMA nods, crying.)*

8. Make Out Session

CAST: JULIA, HALEY
SETTING: School hallway

1 *(At rise, JULIA and HALEY are staring at something down*
2 *the hall.)*
3 **JULIA: I don't think we were supposed to see that.**
4 **HALEY: I doubt it. Kissing is not allowed in school.**
5 **JULIA: But they aren't students.**
6 **HALEY: I have Mr. Richards for math.**
7 **JULIA: I have Mrs. Vick for English.**
8 **HALEY: And they were just ... ooooh!**
9 **JULIA: Making out!**
10 **HALEY: How will I ever sit in math class now and pay**
11 **attention? Mr. Richards will be saying, "What values of**
12 **A and B will make the equation true?" I don't know! All**
13 **I can think about is you and Ms. Vick making out in the**
14 **hallway.**
15 **JULIA: I think it has traumatized us both. Ms. Vick is hard**
16 **and stern in class and to see her slobbering all over**
17 **your math teacher ... Ooooh!**
18 **HALEY: It's just not right. Teachers should never make out.**
19 **Especially at school.**
20 **JULIA: Yeah! They're too old to act that way.**
21 **HALEY: And who would want to kiss Mr. Richards? He's so**
22 **nerdy.**
23 **JULIA: And who would want to kiss Ms. Vick? She's so mean.**
24 **HALEY: It makes you wonder what they see in each other.**
25 **JULIA: I would throw up if I had to kiss Mr. Richards.**
26 **HALEY: I'd rather die.**
27 **JULIA: I think we should tell someone.**
28 **HALEY: Who?**
29 **JULIA: Maybe Mr. Sharp?**

1 HALEY: Tattle to the principal?
2 JULIA: Kissing is not allowed in school. And I think that
3   rule should apply to the teachers as well.
4 HALEY: It should. Especially at the risk of traumatizing
5   their students.
6 JULIA: Look!
7 HALEY: Oh, they're doing it again!
8 JULIA: That's just so wrong.
9 HALEY: School may have let out thirty minutes ago, but
10   that doesn't mean teachers can stand in the hallway
11   and make out after the students leave.
12 JULIA: I wish we'd left.
13 HALEY: Me too. But we had to finish up that stupid collage
14   for art class.
15 JULIA: I know. *(Looking ahead)* Are they ever going to stop?
16 HALEY: Look! The janitor just walked past them.
17 JULIA: I think he thought it was disgusting, too. Did you
18   see the look on his face?
19 HALEY: Boy, they're not stopping for anything.
20 JULIA: Haley, we have to walk down this hall to leave the
21   building. What are we going to do?
22 HALEY: Wait for them to finish? *(Pause as they watch)*
23 JULIA: I don't think it's going to be soon.
24 HALEY: Me, neither.
25 JULIA: Let's do something to make them stop.
26 HALEY: Like what?
27 JULIA: Well, let's start laughing really loud and maybe
28   they'll hear us and stop.
29 HALEY: Good idea. But let's look at each other and
30   pretend we never saw them.
31 JULIA: OK. Ready?
32 HALEY: Ready. *(The GIRLS start laughing.)*
33 JULIA: That is so funny!
34 HALEY: I know!
35 JULIA: Have you ever heard of anything so ridiculous?

1   **HALEY: I haven't! It's the funniest thing I've ever heard!**

2   **JULIA:** *(Laughing)* **Did they stop?**

3   **HALEY:** *(Laughing)* **Let me look.** *(Looks down the hallway*

4   *and stops laughing.)* **No.**

5   **JULIA: Seriously?** *(Looks down the hallway.)* **Wow. They're**

6   **still at it.**

7   **HALEY: I'm never going to look at Mr. Richards the same**

8   **way again.**

9   **JULIA: And I'm never going to look at Ms. Vick the same**

10   **way again, either.**

11   **HALEY: I may need to get transferred out of his class after**

12   **this.**

13   **JULIA: Me too.**

14   **HALEY: Julia, what are we going to do? I'm ready to go**

15   **home.**

16   **JULIA: Me too, but ...** *(Points.)* **How do we get past that?**

17   **HALEY: We could try something else.**

18   **JULIA: What?**

19   **HALEY: Scream.**

20   **JULIA: Scream?**

21   **HALEY: Like we saw a spider or something.**

22   **JULIA: Oh, that's a good idea. Let's try that.**

23   **HALEY: OK. Ready?**

24   **JULIA: Ready!**

25   **HALEY:** *(Points to the floor.)* **Look! A spider!** *(The GIRLS*

26   *scream.)*

27   **JULIA: Oh my gosh! I hate those things!**

28   **HALEY: Oh! Oh! It's huge!**

29   **JULIA: Go away you stupid spider!**

30   **HALEY: Look! It's chasing us!** *(They scream louder.)*

31   **HALEY: Is it working?**

32   **JULIA: I don't know. Let me look.** *(Looks down the hallway,*

33   *then stomps her foot on the floor.)*

34   **HALEY: What are you doing?**

35   **JULIA: I killed the pretend spider. It didn't work.**

1 HALEY: Are they deaf?
2 JULIA: They're definitely in their own little world.
3 HALEY: Why would anyone want to kiss a teacher?
4 JULIA: I wouldn't! Even if I were old enough to kiss a
5   teacher I wouldn't want to. Yuck!
6 HALEY: What now?
7 JULIA: I think we're out of options. Either we wait for
8   eternity or walk past the lovebirds.
9 HALEY: Well, I need to go home.
10 JULIA: Me too.
11 HALEY: I guess we have no choice.
12 JULIA: Just don't look at them when we walk by.
13 HALEY: I'm not looking! I've seen enough. I'm already
14   thinking I might have to see the counselor tomorrow.
15 JULIA: I'll go with you.
16 HALEY: And I think I'm running, not walking down the
17   hall.
18 JULIA: Good idea. I'm going to run for it, too.
19 HALEY: Just don't run into them and for sure don't look.
20 JULIA: I'm not looking, believe me!
21 HALEY: On the count of three ...
22 JULIA and HALEY: One ... two ... three ... *(The GIRLS run off*
23   *screaming.)*

9. Prison

CAST: PIPER, MOM
PROPS: Cell phone, scarf, lipstick. If desired, other
   miscellaneous items on the floor such as clothes, dishes,
   trash, etc.
SETTING: Piper's bedroom

1 **PIPER:** *(Hollers.)* **Then I guess I'll just die in here.**

2 **MOM: Because you refuse to clean your room?**

3 **PIPER: Mom, you just said I couldn't leave my room until I**
4   **cleaned it.**

5 **MOM: That's right.**

6 **PIPER: Mom, I realize it's a little messy —**

7 **MOM:** *(Laughs.)* **A little messy?**

8 **PIPER: OK, maybe more than a little.**

9 **MOM: It's a disaster!**

10 **PIPER: Mom, seriously, it's going to take me weeks to clean**
11   **this room.**

12 **MOM: Then you better get started.**

13 **PIPER: But if I'm not allowed to leave my room for weeks,**
14   **I'm going to die in here. No food, no water ...**

15 **MOM: I'll send some food and water up to your room.**

16 **PIPER: Mom, you'd seriously make me stay in here until it's**
17   **clean?**

18 **MOM: Seriously. School is out. You don't have a job this**
19   **summer. So your job is to clean your room.**

20 **PIPER: And I can't leave my room until it's clean?**

21 **MOM: That's right. I'll have your brother bring you a dinner**
22   **tray to your room tonight.**

23 **PIPER: Mom!**

24 **MOM: And don't get upset, but tonight is lasagna. I know it's**
25   **not your favorite, but oh well.**

26 **PIPER: Can't you fix me a peanut butter and jelly sandwich?**

1   MOM: You'll eat what the family is eating. Or don't eat.
2   PIPER: Do you know what this is, Mom?
3   MOM: *(Looks around the room.)* A disaster. Trash
4   everywhere, clothes strewn about, laundry, papers,
5   half the plates and drinking glasses from the kitchen
6   ... it's a pigsty in here, that's what it is.
7   PIPER: No, it's prison, Mom.
8   MOM: Until you clean your room, yes it is.
9   PIPER: But I have a date with Josh tonight.
10 MOM: I'll let him know that you can't go.
11 PIPER: *You'll* let him know?
12 MOM: That's right. Because you don't have phone
13   privileges while you're in prison.
14 PIPER: You're taking my phone away?
15 MOM: Of course I'm taking your phone away. If I didn't,
16   you'd be in here talking, texting, playing games,
17   everything else besides cleaning your room. So, hand
18   it over.
19 PIPER: Mom! No! Please!
20 MOM: Hand it over!
21 PIPER: *(Hands her the phone.)* I can't believe you're
22   confiscating my phone. This is prison!
23 MOM: Well, you better get busy.
24 PIPER: Mom, are you seriously doing this to me?
25 MOM: *(Looks down at the floor.)* Is that my scarf? *(Picks it*
26   *up.)* It is! I've been looking for this.
27 PIPER: Mom, listen, I don't mind working on my room an
28   hour or two a day, but you can't shut me in here like
29   a prisoner.
30 MOM: Wanna bet?
31 PIPER: I'll call child protective services.
32 MOM: No you won't, because you won't have a phone.
33 PIPER: Then I'll hang out my window and scream for
34   help.
35 MOM: And who's going to save you? The trash man?

1   **PIPER: I'll wave someone down. I'll scream, "Call the**
2   **police! I'm being held hostage!"**
3   **MOM: That's fine. And the minute the police show up, I'll**
4   **escort them to your room and when they see this ...**
5   *(Shakes her head.)* **They might write you a ticket. I'm**
6   **sure it's some sort of health violation.**
7   **PIPER: No they won't.**
8   **MOM: Get busy. I'll have your brother bring some trash**
9   **bags up to your room. Looks like you'll need a lot of**
10   **them.** *(Looks down, then picks something up from the*
11   *floor.)* **What's this?**
12   **PIPER: Lipstick.**
13   **MOM: I thought I lost this.**
14   **PIPER: I borrowed it.**
15   **MOM: Months ago! You borrowed it without permission,**
16   **then what? Tossed it on the floor next to your dirty**
17   **clothes, school notes, and Easter candy wrappers?**
18   **PIPER: I'm sorry.**
19   **MOM: Clean! Now!**
20   **PIPER: But —**
21   **MOM: Or die in here if you want, but you're not coming**
22   **out until it's clean!**
23   **PIPER: But I have a date with Josh in a few hours.**
24   **MOM: Too bad for you, because you're not going.**
25   **PIPER: Wait! Mom! Wait!**
26   **MOM: What?**
27   **PIPER: If by some miracle I get my room clean by tonight,**
28   **can I still go on my date with Josh?**
29   **MOM: If by some miracle. But I'd be amazed.**
30   **PIPER: I can do this. Yes, I will do this. Mom, send up the**
31   **trash bags.** *(Picks up a sheet of paper.)* **Oh look! Here's**
32   **the paper I needed you to sign for Mr. Hoffman's**
33   **class. Oh, never mind. That was last semester. Mom, I**
34   **need those trash bags and fast! Oh, look, there's my**
35   **yearbook. I was looking for that.**

1   MOM: *(Shakes head.)* Good luck. And no stuffing things in
2   drawers or under the bed.
3   PIPER: I won't. It's going to be clean as a whistle. Pizza?
4   .   Where'd that come from?
5   MOM: I'm getting you those trash bags. *(Exits.)*
6   PIPER: My favorite pen! I was looking for this. Wonder
7   where my journal is? Oh, yuck! That's some old
8   cereal and milk. I don't think this bowl is worth
9   saving. *(Hollers.)* Mom, hurry up with those trash
10   bags!

10. Clunker

CAST: ASIA, RILEY
SETTING: Outside Riley's house

1   (*At rise, ASIA and RILEY are standing outside looking at*
2   *RILEY's car.*)
3   ASIA: That's your new car?
4   RILEY: Pretty sad, isn't it?
5   ASIA: What color would you call that?
6   RILEY: Burnt orange?
7   ASIA: Or a bright rusty color. Does it get good gas mileage?
8   RILEY: I don't know. I haven't driven it yet. It won't start.
9   ASIA: It won't start?
10   RILEY: Dad is putting a rebuilt engine in it. It's in bad shape,
11   but fixable for me to drive to school. At least that's what
12   Dad said.
13   ASIA: If it's in such bad shape, why not just buy a new car?
14   Or at a least a newer one than that.
15   RILEY: Because Dad says I'll wreck it before the school year
16   is up. Quoted some teenage driving statistics that I
17   don't remember, but basically said I'd wreck it.
18   Probably total it.
19   ASIA: I'm thinking the sooner the better.
20   RILEY: Then what am I going to drive?
21   ASIA: A new car.
22   RILEY: What new car?
23   ASIA: The new car your dad will buy you after you meet your
24   statistics. Because chances are, after a teen wrecks
25   their first car, they become a much safer driver. I know
26   that for a fact. Of course your insurance goes through
27   the roof, but ... well, it happens.
28   RILEY: No, this is it. Dad said he'd provide me with my first
29   car, but if I wreck it ... or rather, *when* I wreck it, I can

1   buy the next one.

2 ASIA: This is not looking good. Which means you're stuck

3   with driving a burnt orange car to school.

4 RILEY: Or wreck it and drive nothing.

5 ASIA: So once the engine is in place and it's running, it's

6   yours to drive, right?

7 RILEY: *(Frowning as she looks at the car)* **All mine.**

8 ASIA: *(Trying to sound optimistic)* **That's great.**

9 RILEY: I guess it's better than a bike.

10 ASIA: Of course it is.

11 RILEY: But I'd rather have a silver Camaro.

12 ASIA: Who wouldn't? Hey, if ... or after you wreck this car,

13   you could buy a Camaro.

14 RILEY: I couldn't afford that. Or the insurance. Heck, I

15   can't even afford to put the gas in this clunker.

16 ASIA: Ooooh, gas money. How are you going to do that?

17 RILEY: Dad said I had to get a job. He said I need to learn

18   how to be responsible. And he's giving me a head

19   start in life by giving me my new car. If you can even

20   call it a car.

21 ASIA: Well, it still beats riding a bike to school.

22 RILEY: Barely.

23 ASIA: And since you can't afford a silver Camaro ...

24 RILEY: I'm stuck with this.

25 ASIA: Parents can be cruel. My children will have the best

26   of everything.

27 RILEY: Mine too. Is your dad buying you a new car?

28 ASIA: Are you kidding? I'll be working all summer to

29   possibly get a clunker as nice as yours.

30 RILEY: Go to the junkyard. I think that's where Dad got

31   mine. A fixer-upper, he called it. I call it a piece of

32   metal that needs to be melted.

33 ASIA: At least you won't be the only one driving around all

34   embarrassed.

35 RILEY: Talk about not looking cute and amazing.

1   ASIA: But we'll get there.

2   RILEY: Yeah, it'll get me to school all right. I'll just have to

3   duck and run hoping no one sees my car.

4   ASIA: Dang, I'd sure like a red Camaro.

5   RILEY: Silver for me. Maybe one day.

6   ASIA: You know what? I think you will look good driving

7   that car around.

8   RILEY: Oh, right. You think I'll look good driving that

9   clunker?

10 ASIA: I do! Add some cool stickers to the back windshield,

11   hang some cute tassels from the rearview mirror ...

12   Maybe you won't look as hot as you'd look in a silver

13   Camaro, but you'll look good in your car.

14 RILEY: And you know what I think?

15 ASIA: What?

16 RILEY: You're a good liar.

17 ASIA: Hey!

18 RILEY: And a good friend.

19 ASIA: Thanks. Can I have a ride to school when your dad

20   gets it running?

21 RILEY: Of course!

11. Puppet Show

CAST: VANESSA, ISABEL
PROPS: Small paper sacks, markers, paper, pens
SETTING: Classroom

1   *(At rise, VANESSA and ISABEL are drawing faces on their*
2   *paper sacks to use as puppets.)*
3   **VANESSA: It's embarrassing if you ask me.**
4   **ISABEL: I don't understand how putting on a puppet show**
5   **has anything to do with creative writing.**
6   **VANESSA: Because Mrs. Fields said we had to write our own**
7   **stories and make it entertaining to our classmates.**
8   **ISABEL: It's stupid.**
9   **VANESSA: I know. And I don't know what to write about.**
10 **ISABEL: I don't either, but it's a team effort and we've got to**
11 **come up with something.**
12 **VANESSA: Why did you make me sign up for creative**
13 **writing?**
14 **ISABEL: I'm sorry, Vanessa. I don't like this, either.**
15 **VANESSA: I think I'll get some yarn and give my puppet long**
16 **hair.**
17 **ISABEL: Me too. And maybe glue on some material for**
18 **clothes.**
19 **VANESSA: My mom has lots of scrap material we could use.**
20 **ISABEL: Maybe some lace around the neck ...**
21 **VANESSA: I might glue some buttons on for the eyes, then**
22 **draw long eyelashes.**
23 **ISABEL: That'd be cute.**
24 **VANESSA: But we still have one problem.**
25 **ISABEL: What?**
26 **VANESSA: We don't have a story.**
27 **ISABEL: Right. We better get creative and write a story for**
28 **these stupid puppets.**

1   **VANESSA:** *(Picking up a pen)* **Think.**

2   **ISABEL: I'm thinking.**

3   **VANESSA: Let's give them names. That would be a good**
4   **start.**

5   **ISABEL: Uh ... I'm going to name my puppet ... I don't**
6   **know.**

7   **VANESSA: Let's just use our own names.**

8   **ISABEL: Sounds good to me. But it's not very creative.**

9   **VANESSA: Oh well. So what can they say?**

10 **ISABEL:** *(Puts her hand in the sack. As if the puppet is*
11   *speaking)* **Vanessa, you look amazing today.**

12 **VANESSA:** *(Puts her hand in the sack. As if the puppet is*
13   *speaking)* **Thank you, Isabel. So do you.**

14 **ISABEL: I have an idea.**

15 **VANESSA: Is that your puppet speaking or you?**

16 **ISABEL: Me. I need to tell my boyfriend Ryan that it's over,**
17   **so what if I let my puppet break it to him gently? You**
18   **know, work it into the story.**

19 **VANESSA: You want to dump Ryan in front of everyone in**
20   **our creative writing class?**

21 **ISABEL: Well, it wouldn't be me, it'd be my puppet doing**
22   **it. I haven't been able to find the courage in real life,**
23   **so maybe this is my chance to tell him and it gives us**
24   **a story to work with and maybe a good grade for our**
25   **assignment.**

26 **VANESSA: That's not a bad idea. And I could use this**
27   **opportunity to let my puppet tell your boyfriend**
28   **Ryan that I like him.**

29 **ISABEL: What?**

30 **VANESSA: It's true. I've had a huge, mega crush on Ryan**
31   **for like forever.**

32 **ISABEL: Really?**

33 **VANESSA: I hope it's OK.**

34 **ISABEL: Sure. You can have him.**

35 **VANESSA: Thanks!**

1 ISABEL: **Now to write our story.** *(The GIRLS hold up their*
2   *puppets as if they are speaking.)* **So there's this boy ...**
3 VANESSA: **What boy?**
4 ISABEL: **His name is Ryan.**
5 VANESSA: **In our class?**
6 ISABEL: **Yes. That's him.** *(Pointing)* **Over there.**
7 VANESSA: **Isn't he your boyfriend?**
8 ISABEL: **He is.**
9 VANESSA: **I know him. He's very cute.**
10 ISABEL: **Do you think so?**
11 VANESSA: **I do. And he's sweet. But if you have to break up**
12   **with him and move on, I understand where you're**
13   **coming from. But don't worry. I will be there for**
14   **Ryan. He can cry on my shoulder. That is, if he feels**
15   **like crying. But I doubt he will.**
16 ISABEL: **What do you mean, you doubt he will?**
17 VANESSA: **Well, I think I can make him smile. Look. He's**
18   **smiling at me right now.**
19 ISABEL: **No he's not.**
20 VANESSA: **Yes he is.** *(Puts puppet down.)* **OK, not in real**
21   **life, but I'm pretending that he is.**
22 ISABEL: **Oh.** *(Lifts puppet as if it's speaking.)* **Well, I was**
23   **thinking it was time to move on.**
24 VANESSA: **And you should.**
25 ISABEL: **Do you really think I should?**
26 VANESSA: **Yes. Please move on. And thank you for giving**
27   **me this opportunity ... because he's really cute.**
28 ISABEL: **Wait a minute!**
29 VANESSA: *(As if her puppet is flirting)* **Hi, Ryan!**
30 ISABEL: **I've changed my mind.**
31 VANESSA: **No, don't do that.**
32 ISABEL: **I don't want to break up with him anymore.**
33 VANESSA: **Well, maybe he wants to break up with you.**
34   **Move on and make a fresh start. And get to know *me*.**
35 ISABEL: **He's not going to get to know *you*.**

1   VANESSA: But I want him to.

2   ISABEL: But I don't want him to.

3   VANESSA: Isabel, you said you wanted to break up with

4   him.

5   ISABEL: Well, I changed my mind.

6   VANESSA: No, you can't change your mind. You said I

7   could have him!

8   ISABEL: Well, you can't. *(The GIRLS let their puppets fight*

9   *with each other, eventually tearing them up as they do.)*

10   VANESSA: *(After the puppets are ripped)* **Stop! This isn't**

11   going to work.

12   ISABEL: I know.

13   VANESSA: I think we better write a new story.

14   ISABEL: Me too.

15   VANESSA: Do you still want to break up with Ryan?

16   ISABEL: No.

17   VANESSA: Well, I still want you to.

18   ISABEL: Well, I don't want to. *(They pick up the remaining*

19   *pieces of the puppets and throw them at each other.)*

20   VANESSA: Take that!

21   ISABEL: And you take that! And stay away from my

22   boyfriend!

23   VANESSA: So much for this creative writing project!

24   ISABEL: We need a new storyline.

25   VANESSA: And new sacks for our puppets.

12. Lost Phone

CAST: MOLLY, SARA
PROPS: Purse, hall passes, miscellaneous items inside
  purse, cell phones
SETTING: Sara's bedroom

1 *(At rise, SARA is crawling around on the floor looking for*
2 *her phone. MOLLY enters.)*
3 MOLLY: Sara, what are you looking for?
4 SARA: My phone. I thought I set it on the dresser, but it's
5   gone.
6 MOLLY: Let me help you look for it.
7 SARA: I'm dying here. Five minutes without my phone is
8   like ... like being deleted from the world!
9   Communication is gone. I might have received a
10   hundred text messages and I can't read them or reply.
11   My life is horrible. I hate my life. I feel like I can't
12   breathe without my phone.
13 MOLLY: Did you look under the bed?
14 SARA: Yes. I've looked everywhere. *(Stands up.)*
15 MOLLY: Did you look in your purse?
16 SARA: Yes, but I'll look again. *(Takes purse and turns it*
17   *upside down.)*
18 MOLLY: What's with all the hall passes?
19 SARA: I like to take breaks from my classes. Stretch my legs.
20   Go to the bathroom and check my e-mails. You know.
21 MOLLY: Any luck?
22 SARA: No. It's not in my purse. I knew it wasn't because I'd
23   already looked. Oh my gosh, it's nowhere.
24 MOLLY: Well, it didn't grow legs and walk off.
25 SARA: It appears that way.
26 MOLLY: Let's backtrack. When was the last time you saw it?
27 SARA: When I was talking to Ryan on the phone.

1   **MOLLY: Where?**

2   **SARA: At my desk.**

3   **MOLLY: And then you ... ?**

4   **SARA: And then I stood up, went to my dresser, and looked**

5   **at myself in the mirror. I was messing with my hair**

6   **like this.** *(Demonstrates.)*

7   **MOLLY: But between talking to Ryan and messing with**

8   **your hair, what did you do?**

9   **SARA:** *(Still messing with her hair)* **There was nothing in**

10   **between. Do you like my hair up like this?**

11   **MOLLY: That's cute. So you were at your desk talking to**

12   **Ryan and then what did you do when you told him**

13   **good-bye?**

14   **SARA: I think I set my phone on the dresser and then**

15   **started trying out some new hairstyles in front of the**

16   **mirror.** *(Still messing with her hair)* **I'm thinking of**

17   **doing some little curls on the side, then putting the**

18   **rest up like this.**

19   **MOLLY: But Sara, since your phone in not on the dresser,**

20   **where do you think you set it?**

21   **SARA: I don't know, Molly. If I knew that it wouldn't be**

22   **lost.**

23   **MOLLY: Could you have put it in a dresser drawer?**

24   **SARA: No.**

25   **MOLLY: And you didn't leave your room? Didn't go to the**

26   **kitchen for a snack? To the bathroom?**

27   **SARA: No, I didn't go anywhere. I said bye to Ryan then**

28   **walked over here to look at myself in the mirror.**

29   *(Looks in the mirror and smiles.)* **I think I look good**

30   **since I got my braces off.** *(Looking in the mirror, she*

31   *tilts her head and smiles, as if talking to a boy.)* **Hi. Hi!**

32   **Hello!**

33   **MOLLY: Who are you talking to?**

34   **SARA: Just practicing.** *(Tilts head and smiles.)* **Hi. Call me.**

35   **Text me.**

1 **MOLLY: They can't.**
2 **SARA:** *(Still smiling into the mirror)* **Why not?**
3 **MOLLY: Because you lost your phone. Remember?**
4 **SARA:** *(Back to reality)* **Oh, my phone! Where is my phone?**
5 **MOLLY: Did you try calling yourself?**
6 **SARA: Molly, how can I call myself if I don't have a phone**
7 **to call myself with?**
8 **MOLLY: Then I'll call you.**
9 **SARA: It's on vibrate. But maybe we'll hear it buzz.**
10 *(MOLLY calls SARA as SARA looks back at herself in the*
11 *mirror, smiles, and mouths, "Hi." Suddenly, she throws*
12 *her hand to her back pocket.)*
13 **SARA: Found it!**
14 **MOLLY: It's in your back pocket?**
15 **SARA:** *(Smiles.)* **Silly me!**
16 **MOLLY: Seriously? And you never even checked there?**
17 **SARA: Like I said, *silly me*.** *(Looks back in the mirror and*
18 *smiles.)* **Hi. Text me. Call me.**
19 **MOLLY:** *(Shaking her head)* **At least they can now.**

13. Tryouts

CAST: MORGAN, MRS. RIVERS
SETTING: Choir room

1　**MRS. RIVERS: You may begin.**

2　**MORGAN: Now?**

3　**MRS. RIVERS: Now.**

4　**MORGAN:** *(Clears throat.)* **May I have a minute?**

5　**MRS. RIVERS: Morgan, you've had an hour. You asked to go**
6　　　**last. And I hope it's because you want me to think I've**
7　　　**saved the best for last.**

8　**MORGAN: Of course that's what I want you to think.**

9　**MRS. RIVERS: Well then, let's hear it. You may begin.**

10　**MORGAN:** *(Deep breath)* **OK.** *(Another deep breath)* **I'm**
11　　　**almost ready.** *(Another deep breath)*

12　**MRS. RIVERS: Are you nervous?**

13　**MORGAN: Oh, a little. You see, I really want a part in this**
14　　　**musical. It's my all-time favorite. My family has a**
15　　　**tradition of watching it every year around the**
16　　　**Christmas holidays. And afterwards all the cousins, me**
17　　　**included, act out some of the scenes in front of the**
18　　　**adults. So, I've got it all down.**

19　**MRS. RIVERS: That's great.**

20　**MORGAN: I've even got the boys' parts down. I can play a**
21　　　**boy if you need me to.**

22　**MRS. RIVERS: Well, there are many female roles, so I'm**
23　　　**sure if you can sing in tune, you'll have an excellent**
24　　　**chance of receiving one of the female roles.**

25　**MORGAN: Good! But let me just say I'd rather be one of the**
26　　　**kids than a nun. Don't get me wrong, the nuns are**
27　　　**important in the play, but I don't think I'd look great as**
28　　　**a nun, do you? But it's OK. Whatever part you think I**
29　　　**should have will be fine.**

1 MRS. RIVERS: What about the lead?
2 MORGAN: Oh my gosh! I'd love to have the part of Maria!
3   Who wouldn't?
4 MRS. RIVERS: Well, let's see if we saved the best for last ...
5 MORGAN: We did!
6 MRS. RIVIERS: Great. Then let's begin.
7 MORGAN: *(Clears throat.)* **OK.** *(Pause)*
8 MRS. RIVERS: I'm waiting.
9 MORGAN: Do you care what song I sing?
10 MRS. RIVERS: No. Any of the songs will be fine.
11 MORGAN: No preference?
12 MRS. RIVERS: No. But I would like to hear you sing. Today
13   if at all possible.
14 MORGAN: Can I tell you something first?
15 MRS. RIVERS: What's that?
16 MORGAN: I sing in the shower.
17 MRS. RIVERS: That will not help you get a part in the
18   musical.
19 MORGAN: No, I mean I sing *only* in the shower. I'm not
20   sure if I'm a good singer or not because I don't sing in
21   front of other people. Except my relatives at
22   Christmastime, and then all of us cousins sing
23   together so it's not like it's a solo so I'm just not sure.
24 MRS. RIVERS: Not sure?
25 MORGAN: I'm not sure how I sound in real life. You know?
26 MRS. RIVERS: Not really.
27 MORGAN: You know, like on *American Idol?*
28 MRS. RIVERS: I don't watch *American Idol.*
29 MORGAN: OK, so these people walk into a room with all
30   the confidence in the world and they believe they are
31   the best singer in the world and then they sound
32   completely horrible. And the judges are laughing
33   and wondering what that person was thinking. And
34   then the judges try to be nice, but it's hard not to
35   laugh when someone sounds so horrendous ... and I

1   **just don't want to be that person being laughed at**
2   **who didn't have a clue, you know?**
3   **MRS. RIVERS: Not really.**
4   **MORGAN: And one more thing ...**
5   **MRS. RIVERS:** *(Deep breath, frustrated)* **Yes?**
6   **MORGAN: I've never been in choir.**
7   **MRS. RIVERS: That won't be an issue if you can sing.**
8   **MORGAN: And I can't read music.**
9   **MRS. RIVERS: That's not a requirement.**
10   **MORGAN: Oh, good.**
11   **MRS. RIVERS: So let's hear you sing now. Any song from**
12   ***The Sound of Music* will do.**
13   **MORGAN: OK.** *(Deep breath)* **So maybe you'll think I'm a**
14   **natural. Perfectly in tune. The voice of an angel. A**
15   **talent waiting to be discovered. Or ...**
16   **MRS. RIVERS: Or?**
17   **MORGAN: Or you might think I'm bad.**
18   **MRS. RIVERS: Well, let's find out.**
19   **MORGAN: OK.** *(Deep breath)*
20   **MRS. RIVERS: Begin, please.**
21   **MORGAN: Right now?**
22   **MRS. RIVERS: Yes! Now!**
23   **MORGAN: OK.** *(Blurts out, singing badly.)* **"The hills are**
24   **alive with the sound of music ... "**
25   **MRS. RIVERS: Oh no! No, no!**
26   **MORGAN: Wait! Let me try a different song. I was nervous.**
27   *(Deep breath. Sings badly.)* **"Raindrops on roses and**
28   **whiskers on kittens ... "**
29   **MRS. RIVERS: Oh, no! No, my dear.**
30   **MORGAN:** *(Blurts out.)* **"I am sixteen going on seventeen,**
31   **innocent as a rose ... "**
32   **MRS. RIVERS: No, I'm sorry!**
33   **MORGAN:** *(Blurts out.)* **"Climb every mountain, search**
34   **high and low, follow every by-way, every path you**
35   **know ... "**

1   **MRS. RIVERS: No!**

2   **MORGAN: But —**

3   **MRS. RIVERS: No!**

4   **MORGAN: But I'm not good?**

5   **MRS. RIVERS: No!**

6   **MORGAN: Not the best singer you've ever heard?**

7   **MRS. RIVERS: No.**

8   **MORGAN: The worst singer you've ever heard?**

9   **MRS. RIVERS: Yes.**

10 **MORGAN: What?**

11 **MRS. RIVERS: Listen, there are many non-singing parts.**

12 **MORGAN: In a musical?**

13 **MRS. RIVERS: You can be a non-singing nun.**

14 **MORGAN: I thought all the nuns sang.**

15 **MRS. RIVERS: You can be a non-singing nun who moves**

16   **her lips as if she's singing, but nothing comes out of**

17   **her mouth. Do you understand?**

18 **MORGAN: Yes. You want me to do this.** *(As if lip-synching)*

19 **MRS. RIVERS: That's right.**

20 **MORGAN: So I get to run out and tell my friends and**

21   **family I got the part of a non-singing nun?**

22 **MRS. RIVERS: Why don't you just tell them you got a part?**

23 **MORGAN: Are you sure I can't play Maria?**

24 **MRS. RIVERS: Oh, I'm sure.**

25 **MORGAN: But what if you gave me the part of Maria, but**

26   **had someone else who could actually sing behind the**

27   **curtains doing the singing for me? And I could lip-**

28   **synch like you want me to do for the non-singing nun**

29   **part.**

30 **MRS. RIVERS: I've already found a Maria. But you are in**

31   **the musical. You're just not singing.**

32 **MORGAN:** *(Disappointed)* **Great.**

33 **MRS. RIVERS: But I think you'll do an awesome job with**

34   **your acting skills.**

35 **MORGAN: Thanks. I guess.**

1 MRS. RIVERS: So, congratulations. You are one of the
2   nuns.
3 MORGAN: Mrs. Rivers?
4 MRS. RIVERS: Yes, Morgan?
5 MORGAN: Am I the only non-singing nun?
6 MRS. RIVERS: You are.
7 MORGAN: Then I guess I know the truth now.
8 MRS. RIVERS: What truth?
9 MORGAN: I need to keep my singing in the shower!

14. The New Fad

CAST: ASHLEY, MEGAN
SETTING: Outside school

1 ASHLEY: The thing is, if I shave off my eyebrows, then I can
2   pencil in new ones.
3 MEGAN: But why would you do that?
4 ASHLEY: Because it's the latest thing to do. Haven't you
5   heard?
6 MEGAN: No. It is?
7 ASHLEY: Yes. Where have you been?
8 MEGAN: I don't know.
9 ASHLEY: I saw this one girl who penciled in pink eyebrows.
10   It was awesome. But you could use any color.
11 MEGAN: Like orange and black?
12 ASHLEY: Why orange and black?
13 MEGAN: Halloween. Then red and green for Christmas.
14 ASHLEY: You could. The possibilities are endless. Pink,
15   purple, green, metallic —
16 MEGAN: Metallic eyebrows? Strange.
17 ASHLEY: I've seen it and it's really cute.
18 MEGAN: So anyway, you just get a razor and shave off your
19   eyebrows like it's a beard?
20 ASHLEY: Yes.
21 MEGAN: I'd be afraid.
22 ASHLEY: Why?
23 MEGAN: That I wouldn't look good without eyebrows.
24 ASHLEY: But you're going to pencil in new ones.
25 MEGAN: But right now I barely have enough time in the
26   morning to do my makeup and hair, and now I'd have
27   to draw on eyebrows, too? And what if I forgot and went
28   to school without them? It'd be like having a bad hair
29   day, but worse. I'd look scary without any eyebrows.

1 ASHLEY: But when you pencil them in, it looks amazing!
2 MEGAN: Are you going to do it?
3 ASHLEY: I would, but ...
4 MEGAN: What?
5 ASHLEY: My mom would kill me. But I want to.
6 MEGAN: And you've seen this done before?
7 ASHLEY: Yes! Half the girls at Bowie are doing it.
8 MEGAN: Half?
9 ASHLEY: Well, maybe not half, but a lot. Yesterday I saw
10   this girl at the mall who went to Bowie and she'd
11   drawn on hot pink eyebrows.
12 MEGAN: And hers were gone?
13 ASHLEY: Shaved off!
14 MEGAN: *(Feeling her own eyebrows)* Wow.
15 ASHLEY: Everyone was staring at her.
16 MEGAN: I'm sure. So how many other girls have you seen
17   do this?
18 ASHLEY: Just her. But she said everyone was starting to do
19   it. That it was catching on.
20 MEGAN: *(Looks around.)* Not here. All the girls I've seen
21   still have their own eyebrows.
22 ASHLEY: But don't you want to be in style?
23 MEGAN: *(Touching her eyebrows)* No, not really.
24 ASHLEY: Get all the attention?
25 MEGAN: I don't want to be gawked at.
26 ASHLEY: Be a standout? A soul who speaks freedom and
27   change and independence?
28 MEGAN: I'd rather keep a low profile ... and my eyebrows,
29   thank you very much.
30 ASHLEY: Well, I may do it anyway. Shave them off.
31 MEGAN: What about your mom?
32 ASHLEY: It'll be too late by the time she sees me.
33 MEGAN: Then you'll just draw on new eyebrows?
34 ASHLEY: Yes. I'm thinking I'll go with green ... at first. Of
35   course I can change the color each day depending on

1   my mood.

2 MEGAN: Green eyebrows?

3 ASHLEY: Bright green. Then I'll wear green eye shadow so

4   it all blends. Won't that look amazing?

5 MEGAN: Just be sure not to do this. *(Wipes her eyebrows.)*

6   Because then you'll smear them and it'll look weird.

7 ASHLEY: I wouldn't do that.

8 MEGAN: Green eyebrows?

9 ASHLEY: *(Flips hair.)* Call me a fashion expert. A girl who's

10   up on the newest fad. A step ahead of what

11   everyone's yet to catch on to. A fad maker! That's

12   what they'll call me.

13 MEGAN: So you're really going to do it? You're going to

14   shave off your eyebrows and draw on green ones?

15 ASHLEY: Yes.

16 MEGAN: And then show yourself in public?

17 ASHLEY: Yes! I can't wait. "Hello, world. Look at me!" I'll

18   be the talk of the school.

19 MEGAN: Can't argue with that.

20 ASHLEY: Talk about making a fashion statement.

21 MEGAN: Have you ever thought about wearing brown

22   eyebrows?

23 ASHLEY: Brown?

24 MEGAN: For a more natural look.

25 ASHLEY: What would be the point of shaving off my

26   eyebrows only to pencil them back on the same

27   color?

28 MEGAN: True. But the natural look is also a fad too, if I

29   might add.

30 ASHLEY: The natural look is so yesterday. Yes, I think I'll

31   just take my chances with my mom. Besides, what

32   can she do to me after my eyebrows are shaved off?

33 MEGAN: Scream. Maybe cry. But probably scream at you.

34   Oh, and ground you.

35 ASHLEY: Then she'll be glad to see me pencil on my new

1   eyebrows.

2   MEGAN: I doubt that when she sees what color they are.

3   ASHLEY: "Mom, it's the style," I'll tell her.

4   MEGAN: *(As if the mom)* "Ashley, you look hideous!"

5   ASHLEY: "I do not."

6   MEGAN: "Yes, you do. And you know what else?"

7   ASHLEY: "What?"

8   MEGAN: "You're grounded!"

9   ASHLEY: "For how long?"

10   MEGAN: "Until your eyebrows grow back."

11   ASHLEY: "But ... !"

12   MEGAN: And have you thought about that?

13   ASHLEY: Are you still my mom?

14   MEGAN: No.

15   ASHLEY: Thought about what?

16   MEGAN: How ugly you're going to look with stubbly hairs

17   growing back in? Like you have a five o'clock shadow

18   where your eyebrows used to be.

19   ASHLEY: I didn't think about that.

20   MEGAN: My advice ... Don't do it! Ever! Even if half the

21   school ... or just one girl, is doing it. Dare to be

22   different!

23   ASHLEY: Dare to be different? How?

24   MEGAN: By being you!

15. frog legs

CAST: TENESA, RACHEL
PROPS: Paper sack
SETTING: School hallway

1   (At rise, TENESA and RACHEL run onto the stage, and
2   then suddenly stop. TENESA is holding a paper sack.)
3 TENESA: Oh, great. The bell.
4 RACHEL: I knew we wouldn't make it in time.
5 TENESA: No use running now.
6 RACHEL: True. If we're already late, why not take our time?
7 TENESA: Late is late.
8 RACHEL: This is my third tardy for this class.
9 TENESA: It's my fifth.
10 RACHEL: Don't you just start over after your third tardy
11   once you have after-school detention?
12 TENESA: Yes, but Mr. Pruitt likes me and ignored the last
13   two tardies. I walked into class late and he just nodded
14   his head like he understood.
15 RACHEL: Well, let's try that. If he asks, we'll just say we were
16   in the ladies room.
17 TENESA: Mr. Pruitt won't go for that. He'll know if we were
18   in there together we were up to something.
19 RACHEL: Which we were.
20 TENESA: Well, we're not going to tell him that.
21 RACHEL: Maybe we can think of a good excuse to tell him.
22 TENESA: We can try.
23 RACHEL: What do you think?
24 TENESA: I don't know. I've already used up all the good
25   excuses.
26 RACHEL: I've got it!
27 TENESA: What?
28 RACHEL: I'll say I fell down the stairs and twisted my ankle

1   **and you were helping me to class.** *(Holds onto her*
2   *shoulder as she limps.)* **See?**
3   **TENESA: That's not a bad idea. As long as you don't forget**
4   **to limp the whole time.**
5   **RACHEL: And if I get sent to the office to see the nurse, I'll**
6   **just say it feels better.**
7   **TENESA: I think that might work. Let's practice.**
8   **RACHEL: OK.** *(Holds onto TENESA as she limps.)* **Ouch.**
9   **Ouch. Ouch.**
10   **TENESA: Very believable.**
11   **RACHEL: How can Mr. Pruitt count us tardy when I'm**
12   **hurt?**
13   **TENESA: He won't. Just make sure when class is over you**
14   **limp while walking out. Don't forget!**
15   **RACHEL: Right. And you know, to make it more**
16   **believable, you could ask Mr. Pruitt if you could go to**
17   **the office to get an ice pack for me. And on the way to**
18   **the office, you could finish what we couldn't since the**
19   **bell rang.**
20   **TENESA: Alone?**
21   **RACHEL: Well, I can't go with you. I'm hurt!**
22   **TENESA: But what if I get caught?**
23   **RACHEL: Just be careful.**
24   **TENESA: And you won't be there to be my lookout.**
25   **RACHEL: Oh, you'll be fine.**
26   **TENESA: Easy for you to say. You'll be in class getting**
27   **everyone's sympathy and I'll be breaking into**
28   **Shane's locker.**
29   **RACHEL: No one will see you. Do you remember the**
30   **combination?**
31   **TENESA: Twelve-eight-sixteen.**
32   **RACHEL: Good. Meredith is a good friend for sneaking me**
33   **Shane's locker combination.**
34   **TENESA: Do you want me to leave it in the sack or dump it**
35   **out?**

1 RACHEL: Dump it on top of his books.

2 TENESA: I sure hope it doesn't jump out of the locker
3   before I can shut it.

4 RACHEL: It's dead. Remember? Dump it out, slam the
5   door, and run.

6 TENESA: Then run to the office and get you an ice pack
7   for your fake sprained ankle.

8 RACHEL: Exactly!

9 TENESA: I don't know how I got myself into this.

10 RACHEL: By being my BFF. I'd do the same thing for you,
11   Tenesa.

12 TENESA: I know. And I can't stand Shane any more than
13   you can. He's such a jerk.

14 RACHEL: *(Takes the sack from TENESA.)* And we know his
15   weakness and have it right here. *(Looks inside the*
16   *sack.)* Ooooh!

17 TENESA: Fear of frogs.

18 RACHEL: Shane was such a baby when we had to dissect
19   the frog in science class.

20 TENESA: And we didn't even make him feel bad about it.

21 RACHEL: I know! We let him sit back and close his eyes.

22 TENESA: Because we were being nice.

23 RACHEL: Well, I did tease him some. I said he was a baby,
24   but I still didn't deserve what he did to me.

25 TENESA: Fed you frog legs, which you thought were
26   chicken tenders.

27 RACHEL: I threw up!

28 TENESA: I know. I was there.

29 RACHEL: Maybe some people like to eat frog legs, but not
30   me.

31 TENESA: So Shane, who's terrified of frogs, will get one in
32   his locker today.

33 RACHEL: *(Hands the sack back to TENESA.)* Here you go.

34 TENESA: You know, Shane will know who put this in his
35   locker.

1 RACHEL: Of course.

2 TENESA: And then it might start a mad cycle. You'll open

3   your band locker and there will be frogs. Of course

4   he'll have to get someone else to plant them there, but

5   knowing Shane, he will.

6 RACHEL: Right. Or I'll look inside my mailbox and guess

7   what?

8 TENESA: Frogs.

9 RACHEL: Or I'll tear open a package thinking it's from my

10   grandmother and guess what's inside?

11 TENESA: Frogs.

12 RACHEL: It'll be like a horror movie called *Frogs.* In the

13   backseat of my car, in the glove compartment,

14   slipped into my purse, my locker, my backpack ...

15   They'll show up everywhere.

16 TENESA: You know, we could just forget about this and

17   put a stop to it before it gets out of hand.

18 RACHEL: Maybe you're right. I'd hate to dump out my

19   favorite cereal in the morning only to pour milk over

20   a dead frog.

21 TENESA: So I won't put this dead frog in his locker?

22 RACHEL: Yeah, let's forget it.

23 TENESA: But what are we going to do with this? *(Holds up*

24   *the sack.)*

25 RACHEL: Leave it. No one is around.

26 TENESA: *(Sets the sack down.)* Now what about our tardy?

27 RACHEL: *(Holds onto TENESA and limps as they walk.)*

28   Ouch, ouch, ouch ...

29 TENESA: Easy does it. I think I'll ask Mr. Pruitt if I can go

30   to the office and get you an ice pack.

31 RACHEL: Thanks. I think that might help. *(They exit with*

32   *RACHEL limping Off-Stage.)*

16. Mismatched

CAST: AMANDA, MRS. MARRS
PROPS: Tissue, pen, school pass
SETTING: School office

1 AMANDA: Mrs. Marrs, I need to check out of school.
2 MRS. MARRS: Do you have a fever?
3 AMANDA: No.
4 MRS. MARRS: Doctor's appointment?
5 AMANDA: No.
6 MRS. MARRS: Dentist appointment?
7 AMANDA: No.
8 MRS. MARRS: Dermatologist?
9 AMANDA: Does my skin look bad?
10 MRS. MARRS: No, but you are a teen. Pimples popping out
11   right and left. Are you drinking plenty of water? I've
12   heard that it's good for your skin.
13 AMANDA: I don't have an appointment with a
14   dermatologist. But does my skin really look that bad?
15 MRS. MARRS: And keep your hands off your face. No
16   picking and popping ... you know?
17 AMANDA: I'm not seeing a dermatologist.
18 MRS. MARRS: Then are you going to a funeral? Who died?
19   Let me just offer my condolences.
20 AMANDA: No one died.
21 MRS. MARRS: Well, then that just leaves only one thing. You
22   feel like you're going to puke.
23 AMANDA: No!
24 MRS. MARRS: Well, those are all the reasons I allow
25   students to check out of school. Oh, and let me tell you
26   that if your boyfriend broke up with you and you are
27   just wanting to go home to cry, it won't happen. *(Offers*
28   *her a tissue.)* You may cry in class while you do your

1   class work.

2   AMANDA: Mrs. Marrs, my boyfriend didn't break up with

3   me.

4   MRS. MARRS: Then you need to get back to class.

5   AMANDA: What if I need to go home to save myself from

6   further embarrassment?

7   MRS. MARRS: Look, I've heard all the excuses in the world

8   and none have worked so far. And the bad hair day

9   won't work, either. *(As if a teen)* "Mrs. Marrs, I can't

10   stay at school looking like this!"

11 AMANDA: I'm not having a bad hair day. Am I? Does my

12   hair look all right?

13 MRS. MARRS: I'd say it's so-so, but it's not bad enough to

14   get you a pass to go home.

15 AMANDA: So-so?

16 MRS. MARRS: Then what is it? You forgot your homework

17   and you don't want to deal with the repercussions in

18   class?

19 AMANDA: Homework has been completed.

20 MRS. MARRS: Let me think, let me think ...

21 AMANDA: I could just tell you what the problem is.

22 MRS. MARRS: You lost a contact and you don't have a

23   spare one. Well, I say, you can look through your one

24   good eye.

25 AMANDA: I don't wear contacts.

26 MRS. MARRS: You were the last person to leave your

27   house this morning and you're afraid you left your

28   straightener on? And you know what I say? Call a

29   parent. Do you need to use the office phone?

30 AMANDA: No, that's not it.

31 MRS. MARRS: You forgot your lunch money. You can

32   charge it to your account. So, don't worry about it.

33 AMANDA: No!

34 MRS. MARRS: You need to go home to get a book? And I say

35   no siree.

1   AMANDA: All my books are in my locker.
2   MRS. MARRS: Well, you don't have a valid excuse. So you
3   just march right back to class, Missy.
4   AMANDA: But I haven't even told you my excuse.
5   MRS. MARRS: All right. Let's hear it. But make it fast.
6   AMANDA: Somehow, someway, I came to school this
7   morning wearing two different pairs of shoes.
8   MRS. MARRS: Let me see.
9   AMANDA: See.
10 MRS. MARRS: How in the world did you do that?
11 AMANDA: The only thing I can remember is putting on
12   one shoe, then getting a text from Jason that he
13   thinks it's time to go our separate ways. Of course
14   that upset me because I love Jason with all of my
15   heart. So I sent him a text saying that's what I
16   wanted, too.
17 MRS. MARRS: Why would you do that? You just said you
18   loved him with all your heart.
19 AMANDA: I had to lie. Duh!
20 MRS. MARRS: Why? Why didn't you beg him to stay with
21   you?
22 AMANDA: Because I'm not begging any guy to stay with
23   me! Not even Jason.
24 MRS. MARRS: So you were upset and put on the wrong
25   shoe?
26 AMANDA: Well, not right then. After that I got another
27   text from Jason saying he couldn't believe I wanted to
28   break up and he was crushed.
29 MRS. MARRS: So your lying to him worked?
30 AMANDA: Yes, but then I set my phone down and my mom
31   started screaming at me. "You're going to be late for
32   school!" So I grabbed my other shoe, threw it on, and
33   ran out the door.
34 MRS. MARRS: And here you are.
35 AMANDA: Mrs. Marrs, it's embarrassing.

1 MRS. MARRS: I can imagine.

2 AMANDA: So can I check out of school and go home?

3 MRS. MARRS: No.

4 AMANDA: Please! Everyone is laughing at me.

5 MRS. MARRS: So? People get laughed at all the time at
6   school.

7 AMANDA: But I don't like being laughed at.

8 MRS. MARRS: *(Looking at her shoes)* That does look stupid.

9 AMANDA: I know!

10 MRS. MARRS: But you need to get back to class.

11 AMANDA: Mrs. Marrs, please! Can't I run home and
12   change shoes? I'll come back!

13 MRS. MARRS: I'm sorry, but no. You can learn with two
14   mismatched shoes. Your brain doesn't care.

15 AMANDA: But I can't concentrate when I'm embarrassed
16   and being laughed at.

17 MRS. MARRS: Then go barefoot.

18 AMANDA: Barefoot?

19 MRS. MARRS: Take your shoes off and run to class. You
20   can leave your shoes in here if you like.

21 AMANDA: But what's everyone going to say?

22 MRS. MARRS: Who cares what everyone says?

23 AMANDA: *(Raises her hand.)* I do!

24 MRS. MARRS: I'm sorry, but I can't let you go home for
25   mismatched shoes.

26 AMANDA: Are you sure?

27 MRS. MARRS: I'm sure. *(Looks at AMANDA's shoes.)* But
28   that does look stupid. I bet you do get laughed at all
29   day. *(As if a teen)* "Hey, did you notice your shoes don't
30   match?" *(Laughs and points.)*

31 AMANDA: I'm feeling sick.

32 MRS. MARRS: Like you're going to puke?

33 AMANDA: Yes.

34 MRS. MARRS: Oh, in that case, you can go home.

35 AMANDA: I can?

1   **MRS. MARRS: Yes. We don't need any of that around here.**
2   *(Hands her a pass.)* **Here you go. And while you're**
3   **home ... change your shoes.**
4   **AMANDA: Yes ma'am!** *(Exits.)*
5   **MRS. MARRS:** *(Shakes her head.)* **Teenagers.**

17. Germophobic

CAST: HANNAH, JASMINE
SETTING: Bathroom at a restaurant

1 *(At rise, HANNAH and JASMINE are in the bathroom*
2 *looking at themselves in the mirror.)*
3 **HANNAH:** *(Leans forward, looking at her teeth in the mirror.)*
4 **Stupid broccoli. Always gets in my teeth.** *(Uses her nail*
5 *to remove the broccoli.)*
6 **JASMINE:** *(Looking in the mirror, she messes with her hair.)*
7 **Good thing you saw it before the boys did.**
8 **HANNAH: That would've been embarrassing. Hello!** *(Smiles*
9 *in the mirror.)* **Then green stuff stuck between my teeth.**
10 **JASMINE:** *(Smiles in the mirror.)* **I think I'm good. But my**
11 **hair ... I don't know.**
12 **HANNAH: Would it be mean to say I don't like my date?**
13 **JASMINE: You don't like Stanley?**
14 **HANNAH: Jasmine, I know he's you're friend and you set us**
15 **up on this blind date because you thought we were the**
16 **perfect match ... but I'm just not feeling the connection.**
17 **JASMINE: It's all right, Hannah. He's more of Jake's friend**
18 **than mine. Jake said that Stanley can't ever seem to**
19 **find a girlfriend and he thought he'd help.**
20 **HANNAH: Why do you suppose he can't find a girlfriend?**
21 **JASMINE: Because he's a little odd?**
22 **HANNAH: Odd is a good term. Did you notice how he was**
23 **quite belligerent over no one double dipping their**
24 **chips in the salsa?**
25 **JASMINE: I know. Like who really cares about that? I double**
26 **dip all the time. I'm not afraid of a few germs.**
27 **HANNAH: Apparently Stanley is afraid of germs. And did**
28 **you notice the hand sanitizer he had in his pocket?**
29 **JASMINE: I did. I think he pulled it out at least five times**

1   during dinner.

2 HANNAH: I counted eight. And I was only counting

3   because he was sitting next to me.

4 JASMINE: I guess he's one of those germophobic people.

5 HANNAH: Which means I don't have to worry about him

6   trying to kiss me.

7 JASMINE: Probably not.

8 HANNAH: I might sneeze a few times during the movie

9   just to make sure.

10 JASMINE: I bet he won't share his popcorn.

11 HANNAH: Or hold hands.

12 JASMINE: He's probably in the boys bathroom right now

13   scrubbing all the germs off his hands.

14 HANNAH: He's probably one of those people who uses a

15   paper towel to open the bathroom door. Afraid of

16   getting any germs after washing his hands.

17 JASMINE: And finish it all off with more hand sanitizer.

18 HANNAH: You know what the sad part is?

19 JASMINE: What?

20 HANNAH: He's really cute.

21 JASMINE: But odd.

22 HANNAH: Very odd.

23 JASMIME: Maybe you could change him.

24 HANNAH: How?

25 JASMINE: I don't know.

26 HANNAH: Sneeze on him and tell him to man up because

27   he's not going to die over a few germs.

28 JASMINE: Or go out there and plant a big wet sloppy kiss

29   on him.

30 HANNAH: Are you serious?

31 JASMINE: And then he'll be so overtaken with you that he

32   won't care about the germs anymore.

33 HANNAH: I doubt it. He'd probably gargle with the hand

34   sanitizer.

35 JASMINE: Maybe not. You could try.

1   HANNAH: Seriously?

2   JASMINE: What have you got to lose?

3   HANNAH: My date.

4   JASMINE: So? You're not enjoying him anyway. And if he

5   runs off in fear of your germs, then you can go with

6   me and Jake to the movie and he can go home with

7   your germs and wait to get sick. But maybe, just

8   maybe ... little hearts will float above his head and he

9   will become a changed man.

10   HANNAH: Little hearts float above his head?

11   JASMINE: It could happen.

12   HANNAH: So you're saying I should just go out there and

13   give him a kiss?

14   JASMINE: Yes. *(Smiles.)* A sloppy one.

15   HANNAH: I can't ...

16   JASMINE: Then kiss his cheek and see how he responds.

17   HANNAH: I'm seeing hand sanitizer rubbed all over his

18   face.

19   JASMINE: Just try it.

20   HANNAH: All right. I'll do it. *(Looks in the mirror and*

21   *puckers up.)* Maybe I will give him a kiss that he won't

22   forget. Then it's either meant to be ... or the

23   germophobic will run for the hills. *(Makes a kissing*

24   *sound with her lips.)*

25   JASMINE: Good luck.

26   HANNAH: Thanks. *(They both look in the mirror again.)*

27   JASMINE: I think we look good.

28   HANNAH: Me too. And I think I look kissable. *(Makes*

29   *kissing sounds.)*

30   JASMINE: Come on, let's go back out there.

31   HANNAH: *(As they exit)* Blind dates are always interesting,

32   aren't they?

33   JASMINE: Always.

34   HANNAH: *(Hollers out.)* Oh, Stanley ... I have a surprise for

35   you!

18. Secret Crush

CAST: ROSA, CLAIRE
PROPS: Books, paper, pen
SETTING: Library

1   *(At rise, ROSA and CLAIRE cover their faces with books as*
2   *if reading. After a moment, they both peer over the books*
3   *to look across the room.)*
4   **ROSA: He's reading your note!**
5   **CLAIRE:** *(Covers her face.)* **Tell me everything.**
6   **ROSA: He's reading ...**
7   **CLAIRE: And?**
8   **ROSA: Still reading.**
9   **CLAIRE:** *(Peers over her book, then suddenly slams the book*
10 *down.)* **And he crumbled it up and threw it away.**
11 **ROSA:** *(Puts her book down.)* **At least it was an anonymous**
12 **letter.**
13 **CLAIRE: And it meant so much to him that he trashed it?**
14 **ROSA: Claire, he didn't know it was from you. It could have**
15 **been from anyone as far as he knows.**
16 **CLAIRE: Exactly. If some anonymous guy wrote me a letter**
17 **like that, I'd be on cloud nine. And I almost wouldn't**
18 **want to know who it was from because the excitement**
19 **of not knowing ... wondering ... dreaming ... I could live**
20 **on that feeling forever.**
21 **ROSA: Maybe Josh thought it was a joke.**
22 **CLAIRE: I doubt it. He's just not into love and romance.**
23 **ROSA: Or secret crushes.**
24 **CLAIRE: Rosa, should I have signed my name?**
25 **ROSA: No! You expressed your feelings and that was good**
26 **enough.**
27 **CLAIRE: Or bad enough. After all, I got to watch him throw**
28 **my love letter away in the trash.**

1   **ROSA: Some boys just aren't into romance.**

2   **CLAIRE: Rosa, look!**

3   **ROSA: What?**

4   **CLAIRE: Josh is digging my letter out of the trash.**

5   **ROSA: Maybe he thought about it and he liked it after all.**

6   **CLAIRE: Look! He's showing my letter to Kyle. I wonder**

7   **why he's doing that?**

8   **ROSA: Josh probably wants some help figuring out who**

9   **gave him the letter.** *(Suddenly, both GIRLS cover their*

10   *faces with the books for a minute. Slowly, they peer over*

11   *the books when they feel it's safe, and then lower them*

12   *again.)*

13   **ROSA: They looked right over here at us as if they knew.**

14   **CLAIRE: Do you think Josh knows it was me?**

15   **ROSA: How could he?**

16   **CLAIRE: Well, he did see me standing near his table after**

17   **I slipped it in his notebook.**

18   **ROSA: But did he see you?**

19   **CLAIRE: I don't think so.**

20   **ROSA: And if he had, you could've been leaving the letter**

21   **from someone else. You know, like the messenger.**

22   **CLAIRE: That's true. But this isn't getting me anywhere,**

23   **Rosa.**

24   **ROSA: Well, write him another love letter, but sign your**

25   **name on it.**

26   **CLAIRE: But I'm scared.**

27   **ROSA: Of what?**

28   **CLAIRE: Rejection.**

29   **ROSA: Claire, look! Josh is holding up a piece of paper that**

30   **says, "Show yourself to me."**

31   **CLAIRE: Oh my gosh! He wants to know who wrote the**

32   **letter. Rosa, what am I going to do?**

33   **ROSA: He just sat back down.**

34   **CLAIRE: That's because the librarian walked by.**

35   **ROSA: He's writing another message.**

1 CLAIRE: I wonder what it's going to say?
2 ROSA: There. He's standing up again. It's says, "Stand up
3   if it's you."
4 CLAIRE: Oh no! What do I do?
5 ROSA: Stand up, I guess.
6 CLARIE: But what if he looks disappointed that it's me?
7 ROSA: Then you can walk to the bookshelf and grab a
8   book and act like you have no idea why he's staring at
9   you. You can even walk by his table and ask," Why are
10   you staring at me?" Then give him a dirty look.
11 CLAIRE: I guess ...
12 ROSA: He's still standing there with that sign. "Stand up
13   if it's you." *(CLAIRE jumps up. Pause as she stares at*
14   *him.)*
15 ROSA: I think he's happy it's you.
16 CLAIRE: *(Gives him a small wave.)* He's smiling at me.
17 ROSA: I think he winked at you.
18 CLAIRE: What do I do now?
19 ROSA: Sit down!
20 CLAIRE: *(Quickly sits down.)* Now what?
21 ROSA: Now you let him make the first move.
22 CLAIRE: But he's still standing and smiling and ... *(Jumps*
23   *up and hollers.)* It was me!
24 ROSA: Claire, what are you doing?
25 CLARIE: Making sure he knows it was me.
26 ROSA: I think he knows that now! Claire, sit down. Sit
27   down!
28 CLAIRE: *(Sits down.)* He's still smiling. What do I do now?
29 ROSA: Wait.
30 CLAIRE: For what?
31 ROSA: For him to make the first move.
32 CLAIRE: Why?
33 ROSA: Why? Because it's the right thing to do.
34 CLAIRE: *(Stands.)* I'm going over there. This secret crush
35   has been blown wide open, and I've suddenly found

1   my nerves. He's got the cutest smile, don't you think?
2   **ROSA:** Sure.
3   **CLAIRE:** *(Gathers her books.)* **You should try writing an**
4   **anonymous letter. It works! Bye!** *(Exits.)*
5   **ROSA:** *(Pulls out a piece of paper and a pen. Writes.)* **Dear**
6   **Jose, you don't know who I am, but I think you're hot.**

19. Backflips

CAST: BRIANNA, ANDREA
SETTING: School gym

1 (At rise, ANDREA is attempting to do the splits when
2 BRIANNA walks in.)
3 BRIANNA: Andrea, what are you doing?
4 ANDREA: I'm trying to do the splits.
5 BRIANNA: Why?
6 ANDREA: Because I've decided to get into gymnastics.
7 (Stretching) I need to be more limber. Ouch!
8 BRIANNA: Why do you want to get into gymnastics?
9 ANDREA: Because Brianna, I'm not involved in anything at
10 school. You're in choir, a member of the pep squad, and
11 on the swim team. What do I do? Nothing.
12 BRIANNA: But gymnastics?
13 ANDREA: (Attempts to do the splits again.) I think I'd be good
14 at it. After I get into shape. Ouch!
15 BRIANNA: Andrea, you're going to be sore tomorrow.
16 ANDREA: I don't care. Now I need to figure out how to do a
17 backflip. Do you know how?
18 BRIANNA: I can't do a backflip! And don't you think you
19 should try a front flip first? Or better yet, try a
20 somersault. When was the last time you did that?
21 ANDREA: I don't know. Kindergarten?
22 BRIANNA: Uh-huh.
23 ANDREA: But those backflips they do on the floor mats look
24 so easy. I want to run across that blue mat and flip, flip,
25 flip! (Jumps up in her excitement and falls down.)
26 BRIANNA: I think you're going to fall, fall, fall!
27 ANDREA: And then I'll learn how to master them on the
28 balance beam.
29 BRIANNA: Andrea, have you ever been on a balance beam?

1   ANDREA: No, but it looks easy. I know, let's pretend there's
2   one right here in front of me. *(Tries to walk straight,*
3   *but wobbles. Jumps up, stretching her legs out, but falls*
4   *down when she does this.)* **Ouch!**
5   BRIANNA: Are you all right?
6   ANDREA: Yes. I need to practice, don't I?
7   BRIANNA: Andrea, most everyone who's in gymnastics
8   started when they were little. Like five years old.
9   You're kind of getting a late start to this.
10 ANDREA: Brianna, I'm determined to do this! I just have
11   to practice hard every day. Maybe all night, too. So I
12   need to start with stretching. *(Stretches.)* **Ouch!** That
13   hurt.
14 BRIANNA: Andrea, I remember you telling me awhile
15   back that you couldn't even do a cartwheel.
16 ANDREA: Maybe I never got that down, but I'm going to.
17   And I believe if you set your mind to do something,
18   then you can do it. Don't you?
19 BRIANNA: I guess.
20 ANDREA: First I'm going to picture myself doing a
21   cartwheel. *(She closes her eyes. A pause.)* **Got it! Now to**
22   prove my point, I'm going to do a cartwheel for you.
23   *(Attempts to do a cartwheel, but it is awkward and her*
24   *legs don't make it up in the air. She falls down.)* **OK, I**
25   need to practice that.
26 BRIANNA: Andrea, give it up.
27 ANDREA: No, Brianna! I can do this. *(Closes her eyes.)* **OK,**
28   think hard. Picture myself doing a cartwheel.
29   *(Attempts another cartwheel, and again it's awkward*
30   *and she falls down.)*
31 BRIANNA: You're going to hurt yourself, Andrea.
32 ANDREA: *(Becoming angry)* **No I'm not! I just need to get**
33   into better shape. I need to stretch. *(Stretches.)* **Ouch!**
34   I can do this. *(Stretches.)* **Ouch!**
35 BRIANNA: Then it's going to take some time. You won't get

1   there overnight.

2 ANDREA: I bet you that by next week I'll be doing those

3   backflips on the balance beam.

4 BRIANNA: OK.

5 ANDREA: OK?

6 BRIANNA: I'll bet you. How much? A hundred dollars?

7   *(Offers her hand.)*

8 ANDREA: I'm not betting any money. It was just a saying.

9 BRIANNA: Well, I tell you what ... I will clap the loudest

10   when you do your backflip on the balance beam.

11 ANDREA: Thank you. I sure hope I make the gymnastics

12   team. Tryouts are next week.

13 BRIANNA: Well, you just never know ...

14 ANDREA: I better get back to stretching.

15 BRIANNA: Yes, you should.

16 ANDREA: *(Stretches.)* Ouch! Dang it! Wow, that really hurt.

17 BRIANNA: And tomorrow when you can't walk, call me

18   and you can come over and soak in the hot tub at my

19   house.

20 ANDREA: I'll be fine.

21 BRIANNA: Good luck.

22 BRIANNA: *(As she attempts to do the splits)* Thanks. Ouch!

23   Man, that hurts!

20. Mother's Day

CAST: CASSIE, JENNA
PROPS: Paper, pens
SETTING: Classroom

1   *(At rise, CASSIE and JENNA sit at their desks staring at*
2   *blank pages of paper.)*
3   CASSIE: This is a stupid assignment.
4   JENNA: It's elementary.
5   CASSIE: I'd rather be doing the plaster of paris thing with
6   an imprint of my hand.
7   JENNA: My mom has like three of those from me.
8   CASSIE: Or a homemade card would be OK. But a letter?
9   JENNA: And spelling does count toward our grade.
10 CASSIE: What's Mrs. Watson going to do? Correct our bad
11   spelling with a red pen and let us give it to our mothers
12   on Mother's Day? I'd probably get a bad grade. I'm
13   terrible at spelling. Then I'd give my mom her Mother's
14   Day letter and I'd get in trouble at the same time.
15 JENNA: Yeah! "Sorry, Mom, I made a fifty-five on your
16   Mother's Day letter."
17 CASSIE: Really! And besides all that, I don't know what to
18   say.
19 JENNA: "Dear Mom, Thanks for ruining my life."
20 CASSIE: Yeah! For interfering with everything I want to do.
21 JENNA: Demanding to know the details.
22 CASSIE: Setting curfews.
23 JENNA: Telling me no.
24 CASSIE: Telling me no like all the time!
25 JENNA: Forcing family nights on me.
26 CASSIE: Telling me who I can and can't hang out with.
27 JENNA: All your stupid rules, Mom!
28 CASSIE: And Mom, I can't wait to get out of here.

1 JENNA: And me having to write you a letter to tell you how
2   much I love you is torture. Pure torture!
3 CASSIE: Sure, I loved you when I was five years old.
4 JENNA: Maybe even until I started junior high, but after
5   that ... ?
6 CASSIE: You just had to start getting into my business.
7 JENNA: You know what I want to say?
8 CASSIE: Are you talking to your mom or me?
9 JENNA: My mom. I want to say, "Hey Mom, you stay out of
10   my life and I'll stay out of yours."
11 CASSIE: Yeah, because it's my life.
12 JENNA: So leave me alone.
13 CASSIE: Yeah! Leave me alone!
14 JENNA: I'm never having kids.
15 CASSIE: Me neither.
16 JENNA: It's so stupid! We have to write a love letter to our
17   moms for Mother's Day. For a grade, too!
18 CASSIE: I'd rather write a love letter to my dog.
19 JENNA: *(Taps pen on desk.)* I don't know what to say.
20 CASSIE: Me neither.
21 JENNA: "Hey Mom, thanks for cooking my favorite dinner
22   for me last night." Well, that's all I can think of to say.
23 CASSIE: Jenna, it has to be two pages. At least.
24 JENNA: Then I'm going to write really big.
25 CASSIE: Let's see ... How about this? "Mom, I appreciate
26   you loaning me twenty dollars for the book I lost
27   even though you're making me pay you back. I'm
28   sure you're teaching me a lesson on responsibility.
29   Thanks, Mom." But that's not even close to two pages.
30 JENNA: I thought of something. "Mom, thanks for staying
31   with me in my room all night when I was sick."
32   That's a nice thing to say, isn't it?
33 CASSIE: That's good. And my mom brought me cold
34   washrags for my head when I was sick. And chicken
35   soup.

1 JENNA: And she did buy me those shoes I had to have.

2 CASSIE: My mom took me to the movies when I was
3   having a bad weekend. Everyone was busy and I was
4   feeling left out and lonely. But ... Mom was there.

5 JENNA: That's something good to write about. My mom
6   stayed up with me half the night to help me finish a
7   stupid science project that I waited until the last
8   minute to do.

9 CASSIE: That's something good to write about, too. *(Pause*
10   *as they write)*

11 JENNA: I guess I do love my mom.

12 CASSIE: Yeah, I guess I love my mom, too.

13 JENNA: But she still makes me mad.

14 CASSIE: I know! My mom, too. *(Pause as they write)*

15 JENNA: How do you spell "infinity"?

16 CASSIE: Heck if I know. You'll have to look it up. Is that
17   how much you love your mom?

18 JENNA: Yeah.

19 CASSIE: Me too.

20 JENNA: But it's still a stupid assignment.

21 CASSIE: It's wrong, that's what it is.

22 JENNA: *(Looking at her paper)* Sure, I loved you when I was
23   five ...

24 CASSIE: *(Looking at her paper)* Maybe until I started junior
25   high ...

26 JENNA: But after that ... ?

27 CASSIE: After that ... ?

28 JENNA: I've always loved you, Mom! Wouldn't admit it
29   most the time.

30 CASSIE: I love you, Mom. You're always there for me. The
31   one person I can count on.

32 JENNA: When I thought everyone in the entire school
33   hated my guts, you assured me they didn't.

34 CASSIE: You give me hugs, encouragement ... love.

35 JENNA: *(Sniffles.)* And that one day I messed up my hair by

1   mixing three colors of dye then putting it on ... it was
2   horrible. I was hideous! But you rushed me to your
3   hairdresser and saved the day.
4 CASSIE: And Mom, you never missed one softball game.
5   And you always clapped the loudest. I would've been
6   so sad if you hadn't been there.
7 JENNA: *(Sniffling and writing)* I love you, Mom!
8 CASSIE: *(Wiping her eyes)* I love you, Mom.
9 JENNA: Maybe this won't be so hard after all.
10 CASSIE: It might even be longer than two pages.
11 JENNA: I'm going to color red hearts on mine.
12 CASSIE: Good idea.
13 JENNA: How do you spell "spectacular"?
14 CASSIE: I don't have a clue. *(They continue writing.)*

21. All Wrapped Up

CAST: NANCY, RAVEN
PROPS: Box, newspaper, tape, scissors
SETTING: Department store

1   *(At rise, RAVEN is interviewing for a gift wrapping job.)*

2   **NANCY: Do you have any previous experience?**

3   **RAVEN: I've wrapped presents during the holidays.**

4   **NANCY: At what store did you wrap gifts?**

5   **RAVEN: Oh, not at a store, but at my house. For my mom.**

6   **Usually while sitting in front of the TV watching reruns**

7   **of *The Brady Bunch*. I love that show. Don't you?**

8   *(Begins to sing.)* **"Here's the story of a lovely lady, who**

9   **was bringing up three very lovely girls — "**

10 **NANCY: Stop!**

11 **RAVEN: I'm sorry. That song just makes me happy.**

12 **NANCY: So you're telling me that you don't have any**

13   **previous experience as a gift-wrapper? Other than**

14   **wrapping gifts on your living room floor?**

15 **RAVEN: That's correct. But I'm friendly.**

16 **NANCY: You don't have to be friendly to wrap gifts. You have**

17   **to be quick.** *(Snaps fingers.)*

18 **RAVEN: I can be quick. I can wrap as fast as they come. Like**

19   **this.** *(Moves her hands in a fast motion as if wrapping a*

20   *gift.)* **See?**

21 **NANCY: And you must be detailed. No sloppiness is**

22   **acceptable.**

23 **RAVEN: Oh, of course! A gift needs to be presented at its very**

24   **best.**

25 **NANCY: That's right.**

26 **RAVEN: Last Christmas, I wrapped all the gifts at my house.**

27   **Except for mine of course. Very professionally done, if**

28   **you ask me.**

1 NANCY: Well, that's what we are looking for. A
2   professional gift wrapper. And with fourteen
3   applicants for this job, I want to make sure I pick the
4   very best.
5 RAVEN: That would be me!
6 NANCY: Well, then, you must demonstrate to me your
7   creative ability. Here's a box, newspaper, tape, and
8   scissors. Show me your very best work with these
9   simple materials.
10 RAVEN: You want me to wrap this box in newspaper?
11 NANCY: That's right.
12 RAVEN: I do that when I'm in a bind and I don't have any
13   wrapping paper, but for a store like this ... ?
14 NANCY: It's a test.
15 RAVEN: Oh, I see.
16 NANCY: I'll step away while you wrap the box. And I will
17   be timing you, as being fast is part of this job as well.
18 RAVEN: You're going to time me? Oh, that's a lot of
19   pressure.
20 NANCY: Please let me know when you are finished. You
21   may begin. *(Steps back.)*
22 RAVEN: How hard can this be? *(Quickly wraps the box as*
23   *she sings.)* "Here's the story of a lovely lady, who was
24   bringing up three very lovely girls ... " I wonder how
25   I'm supposed to make a bow? *(Crumbles up paper and*
26   *sticks it on top of the box.)* Finished!
27 NANCY: *(Steps forward and looks at her watch.)* That was
28   fast.
29 RAVEN: I'm as fast as they come.
30 NANCY: *(Looks at the package.)* That ... that ...
31 RAVEN: Do you like it? .
32 NANCY: That is horrendous!
33 RAVEN: Are you serious? Well, it would've looked better if
34   you'd given me some pretty paper instead of
35   newspaper.

1   NANCY: I was expecting a tightly-wrapped gift with neat
2   and even folds on the ends. But this looks like a five-
3   year-old wrapped it.
4   RAVEN: Can I have another chance?
5   NANCY: No, I'm afraid not.
6   RAVEN: But I work better with real wrapping paper.
7   NANCY: Our customers expect professionally-wrapped
8   gifts. If I let you hand over something like that, I'd
9   lose my job.
10 RAVEN: But —
11 NANCY: Interview is over!
12 RAVEN: But —
13 NANCY: You're not what we're looking for.
14 RAVEN: Fine. But let me do one thing first.
15 NANCY: What?
16 RAVEN: *(Unwraps the gift.)* It's just what I wanted! Thank
17   you! Thank you so much!
18 NANCY: *(Glaring at her)* There's nothing in that box.
19 RAVEN: I know. But I realized I like unwrapping gifts
20   more than I like wrapping gifts, so thanks for not
21   hiring me.
22 NANCY: This interview is over.
23 RAVEN: Thank goodness. What was I thinking? Wrapping
24   gifts is boring. But unwrapping them is the fun part!
25   *(Sings as she exits.)* "Here's the story of a lovely lady,
26   who was bringing up three very lovely girls ... "

Two Men

22. 3-Second Memory

CAST: KYLE, ERIC
PROPS: Book
SETTING: Library

1　*(At rise, KYLE is attempting to memorize a monologue*
2　*when ERIC enters.)*
3　**KYLE:** *(Slams book down.)* **I can't do this.**
4　**ERIC:** *(Enters.)* **Hey, what's wrong?**
5　**KYLE: No one understands me. Except for Pete.**
6　**ERIC: Who's Pete?**
7　**KYLE: My goldfish.**
8　**ERIC: Your goldfish is the only person ... well, fish ... who**
9　**understands you?**
10　**KYLE: Yes.**
11　**ERIC: Why?**
12　**KYLE:** *(Picks up the book.)* **Have you ever tried to memorize**
13　**a monologue?**
14　**ERIC: Uh ... no. And I don't ever plan to, either. And Kyle, do**
15　**you remember I tried to talk you out of signing up for**
16　**drama?**
17　**KYLE: But I like drama. I like acting. I'm good at it. I'm just**
18　**terrible at memorizing lines.**
19　**ERIC: Question. How does Pete, your goldfish, understand**
20　**that?**
21　**KYLE: Simple. Goldfish only have a memory span of three**
22　**seconds.**
23　**ERIC: I didn't know that.**
24　**KYLE: I read it somewhere. And that's good because**
25　**otherwise how could you swim around the same**
26　**fishbowl all day long without going nuts?**
27　**ERIC: That's interesting. So, like every three seconds, Pete**
28　**loses his memory and everything is new all over again?**

1   *(Imitates a fish.)* **I don't think I've ever been here**
2   **before.**

3   **KYLE: But hello, Pete! You've been in that fishbowl for a**
4   **year.**

5   **ERIC: I'd like to have a three-second memory when I'm in**
6   **calculus because I hate being in there.**

7   **KYLE: No you wouldn't.**

8   **ERIC: Yeah, I would. Maybe I could stand Mr. Carson's**
9   **class then. Find the largest possible volume of a right**
10   **circular cylinder that is inscribed in a sphere of**
11   **radius r. Heck if I know! Oh, I hate that class.**

12   **KYLE: And I can't memorize my lines for this monologue**
13   **because I've got a three-second memory like Pete.**

14   **ERIC: How about writing it on your palm? That way if you**
15   **forget your line, you can glance at your hand.**

16   **KYLE: Eric, do you think I can write six hundred or so**
17   **words on my hand?**

18   **ERIC: That much?**

19   **KYLE: It's a monologue.**

20   **ERIC: So how much have you memorized so far?**

21   **KYLE: A few lines.**

22   **ERIC: Let me hear it.**

23   **KYLE: OK.** *(Clears throat.)* **My parents are ruining my life!**

24   **ERIC: In real life or is that your monologue?**

25   **KYLE: It's my monologue.**

26   **ERIC: Oh, sorry. Start over.**

27   **KYLE: OK.** *(Clears throat.)* **My parents are ruining my life!**

28   **ERIC: Why did you stop?**

29   **KYLE: Because I forgot the rest.**

30   **ERIC: Man! Here. Give me your book and I'll help you.**

31   **KYLE:** *(Hands him the book. Points.)* **Right here.**

32   **ERIC: Start over and I'll help you.**

33   **KYLE: OK.** *(Pause)* **My parents ... my parents ...**

34   **ERIC: Keep going.**

35   **KYLE: My parents ...**

1 ERIC: Are ruining ...
2 KYLE: Oh yeah! My parents are ruining my life!
3 ERIC: Keep going.
4 KYLE: Uh ... uh ...
5 ERIC: How ...
6 KYLE: How? I don't know how. I forgot!
7 ERIC: No. *How* is the next word.
8 KYLE: How is the next word?
9 ERIC: Yes. Start over and maybe you'll remember.
10 KYLE: OK. I'll try.
11 ERIC: Go ahead.
12 KYLE: Uh ... uh ...
13 ERIC: My ...
14 KYLE: My ...
15 ERIC: Parents ...
16 KYLE: Parents ...
17 ERIC: My parents ...
18 KYLE: My parents ...
19 ERIC: Kyle, come on! Don't you remember?
20 KYLE: No! I told you I have the memory of a goldfish.
21 ERIC: Come on! You can do this. My parents ...
22 KYLE: My parents ... *(Suddenly)* are ruining my life!
23 ERIC: Good. Go on.
24 KYLE: And ...
25 ERIC: Not and, how ...
26 KYLE: How ...
27 ERIC: How might you ask?
28 KYLE: I don't have a clue.
29 ERIC: Kyle! That's the next line.
30 KYLE: See! I can't remember how his parents are ruining
31   his life.
32 ERIC: *(Shakes head.)* You're right.
33 KYLE: About what?
34 ERIC: You do stink at memorizing.
35 KYLE: I told you! So what am I going to do?

1   **ERIC: You want my advice?**

2   **KYLE: Yes.**

3   **ERIC: Schedule change ASAP!** *(Exits.)*

4   **KYLE: But I like drama. I'm good at drama. I'm just bad at**

5   **memorizing. Let me try this again.** *(Takes a deep*

6   *breath.)* **"My parents are ruining my life!" Yeah, that's**

7   **it. And ... and ... and heck if I know why! Maybe for**

8   **giving birth to a son who has a three-second memory.**

9   *(Shakes head.)* **I should've been born a goldfish**

10 **instead.**

23. Do You Want Fries with That?

CAST: JARED, TYLER
PROPS: Paper and pen for taking lunch order
SETTING: Fast food restaurant

1 (At rise, JARED is taking TYLER's order at a fast food
2 restaurant.)
3 JARED: Do you want fries with that?
4 TYLER: Why do you people always ask that question?
5 JARED: It's part of my job.
6 TYLER: Don't you think if I wanted fries with my order I
7   would've ordered fries?
8 JARED: (Shrugs.) Maybe you forgot.
9 TYLER: I'm ordering my own lunch. How could I forget?
10 JARED: How could you not?
11 TYLER: Excuse me?
12 JARED: How could you not want French fries with that
13   order? Warm, salty fries dipped in catsup. Yum!
14 TYLER: Maybe I'm watching my weight.
15 JARED: By ordering a double cheeseburger? That's already a
16   day's worth of calories, so why not make it good and get
17   a super-sized order of fries with it?
18 TYLER: Why don't you stop worrying about my calories you
19   moron and get my order!
20 JARED: Did you say you wanted to super size that order?
21 TYLER: No!
22 JARED: But don't you want to make it a combo so you can
23   have fries, too?
24 TYLER: No, I don't.
25 JARED: Are you sure?
26 TYLER: How many times do I have to tell you I don't want
27   fries?

1 JARED: I was just asking. I'm sorry. But seriously, who
2   orders a cheeseburger without fries?
3 TYLER: Me!
4 JARED: Strange. Very strange. So, that was one double
5   cheeseburger, minus the onions, correct?
6 TYLER: Yes.
7 JARED: Did you want pickles?
8 TYLER: I only cut the onions.
9 JARED: With pickles and lettuce?
10 TYLER: Yes.
11 JARED: Tomatoes?
12 TYLER: Yes! Do I really have to answer all these questions
13   after telling you to only cut the onions?
14 JARED: Well, I didn't want to mess up your order. Some
15   customers can be quite difficult and get real unhappy
16   fast.
17 TYLER: *(Frowning)* Tell me. Do I look unhappy?
18 JARED: Yes.
19 TYLER: Well, I am because of all your stupid questions.
20 JARED: I'm sorry. I'm just trying to make sure I get your
21   order right.
22 TYLER: And you've got it right ... right?
23 JARED: I believe so. Oh, did you want to add an apple pie
24   with your order for only a dollar?
25 TYLER: No.
26 JARED: But they're on sale. But only for today.
27 TYLER: No!
28 JARED: So that's a double cheeseburger with lettuce,
29   tomatoes, and pickles and cut the onions?
30 TYLER: Yes. That's it.
31 JARED: Did you want fries with that?
32 TYLER: No! Didn't we already go through this?
33 JARED: But how can you refuse? Crispy, salty —
34 TYLER: Listen here, you moron! I — don't — want — fries!
35 JARED: *(Casually)* It's your decision. Sad as it may be. But

1   I'm wondering ... don't you like fries?

2 TYLER: That's not the point.

3 JARED: Because you're like the only person who's come in

4   here today and ordered a burger without fries.

5 TYLER: And I bet it's because if they had tried to order a

6   burger without fries you made them feel guilty about

7   it until they ordered them.

8 JARED: *(Smiles.)* It is my job.

9 TYLER: To make customers feel guilty?

10 JARED: To sell fries.

11 TYLER: Well, you didn't score with me, did you?

12 JARED: And you said no to the apple pie?

13 TYLER: Yes.

14 JARED: Yes you want the apple pie?

15 TYLER: No!

16 JARED: You don't want the apple pie?

17 TYLER: Yes!

18 JARED: Yes?

19 TYLER: No!

20 JARED: Yes? No? What is it? They're on sale, but only for

21   today.

22 TYLER: That's it! I've had it. Just give me my order.

23 JARED: No apple pie?

24 TYLER: Yes! I mean, no!

25 JARED: No?

26 TYLER: *No apple pie!*

27 JARED: *(Smiles, calmly.)* OK, I think we've completed your

28   order.

29 TYLER: Thank you, thank you, thank you!

30 JARED: One double cheeseburger, cut the onions.

31 TYLER: That's correct.

32 JARED: And did you want fries with that?

33 TYLER: *(Takes a deep breath as if he's about to scream, then*

34   *calmly)* Yes.

35 JARED: *(Smiles.)* Yes?

1   **TYLER: Yes.**

2   **JARED: Perfect. I'll be right back with your order.** *(Exits.)*

3   **TYLER:** *(Hollers.)* **And I'll take an apple pie, too! How about**

4   **that?**

24. Fake Flowers

CAST: TREVER, RASAUN
PROPS: Artificial flowers
SETTING: School hallway

1   *(At rise, RASAUN is holding a bouquet of artificial*
2   *flowers. TREVER enters.)*
3   **TREVER: Who are the fake flowers for?**
4   **RASAUN: Jasmine.**
5   **TREVER: Another fight?**
6   **RASAUN: A whopper.**
7   **TREVER: What did you do?**
8   **RASAUN: What did *I* do?**
9   **TREVER: Yeah. What did *you* do?**
10   **RASAUN: Why do you assume it was me?**
11   **TREVER: Because you're the one holding the flowers.**
12   **RASAUN: Well, it wasn't me.**
13   **TREVER: Then what does Jasmine *think* you did wrong?**
14   **RASAUN: She thinks I hang out with the guys more than**
15   **her.**
16   **TREVER: Well, that's true.**
17   **RASAUN: No it's not.**
18   **TREVER: Rasaun, you've been at my house or Jake's house**
19   **every night this week.**
20   **RASAUN: Because it was the battle of *Armageddon*.**
21   **TREVER: I love that game.**
22   **RASAUN: Me too! And Jasmine needs to understand that I**
23   **have hobbies and she has hobbies, so ... And she could**
24   **care less about video games, so what's a guy to do?**
25   **TREVER: Spend all his free time at his friend's house**
26   **playing *Armageddon*?**
27   **RASAUN: I'm not asking her to join me.**
28   **TREVER: I think Jasmine is crying for attention.**

1   **RASAUN: Oh, she's crying all right!** *(Imitates her.)* **"You**
2   **never spend time with me! All you care about is your**
3   **stupid games! I don't even understand the point of**
4   **our relationship anymore if we're never going to**
5   **spend time together!"**
6   TREVER: And you said?
7   RASAUN: I said, "I like to play games with the guys. What's
8   wrong with that?"
9   TREVER: Wrong answer. I bet she dumped you, didn't she?
10   RASAUN: Yeah, she dumped me.
11   TREVER: And you're standing here waiting to give her
12   *fake* flowers? *(Shakes head.)* Dude ...
13   RASAUN: I want to make up with her.
14   TREVER: Fake flowers?
15   RASAUN: I was a little short on cash.
16   TREVER: Where did you get those?
17   RASAUN: From a friend.
18   TREVER: What friend?
19   RASAUN: Actually, a relative.
20   TREVER: Who?
21   RASAUN: Uncle Homer.
22   TREVER: But Uncle Homer is dead.
23   RASAUN: I know.
24   TREVER: You stole those from his grave?
25   RASAUN: He didn't care.
26   TREVER: How do you know?
27   RASAUN: Well, he didn't object.
28   TREVER: That's because he's dead.
29   RASAUN: I know. And since he's dead he doesn't know that
30   I stole these flowers from his grave.
31   TREVER: How do you know? *(Looks heavenward.)* Uncle
32   Homer, I'm sorry for what your nephew did. So
33   disrespectful. But he was desperate. Please forgive
34   him.
35   RASAUN: *(Quickly looks up.)* Yeah, please forgive me. *(To*

1   *TREVER)* Trever, he doesn't know.

2   TREVER: Let's just hope not.

3   RASAUN: Well, anyway, I'm hoping to make up with
4   Jasmine.

5   TREVER: Good luck.

6   RASAUN: You think she'll take me back?

7   TREVER: Maybe if you promise to start spending time
8   with her.

9   RASAUN: I can do that.

10   TREVER: And not just promise, but really do it.

11   RASAUN: I will. So you think she'll forgive me?

12   TREVER: I don't know. You know how girls are ...

13   RASAUN: Difficult.

14   TREVER: Rasaun, can I offer you some advice?

15   RASAUN: Sure.

16   TREVER: Fresh flowers.

17   RASAUN: But I'm broke.

18   TREVER: If you love her, you'll find a way.

19   RASAUN: You're right. I'll ask my mom for a loan.

20   TREVER: And one more word of advice.

21   RASAUN: Yeah?

22   TREVER: Take the fake flowers back to Uncle Homer.
23   Please. *(Looks heavenward.)* He wasn't thinking. He
24   just wasn't thinking.

25   RASAUN: *(Looks up.)* Sorry Uncle Homer. But it was for a
26   good cause. *(To TREVER)* Do you really think he
27   cared?

28   TREVER: You never know.

29   RASAUN: Anyway, I'm taking these flowers back to the
30   cemetery.

31   TREVER: Hey, are you playing *Armageddon* with us
32   tonight?

33   RASAUN: Of course! I'm not missing that.

34   TREVER: But what about Jasmine?

35   RASAUN: I don't know. *(Looks heavenward.)* Tell me what

1   to do, Uncle Homer. *(A pause)*

2 TREVER: Did he say anything?

3 RASAUN: *(A bit disappointed)* Yeah ...

4 TREVER: What?

5 RASAUN: He told me to go ahead and give her these fake

6   flowers then I could play all the video games I

7   wanted.

8 TREVER: Then you better listen to him. And hey, you can

9   say you tried and she wouldn't work things out with

10   you.

11 RASAUN: Right. Can't blame a guy for trying.

12 TREVER: See you tonight.

13 RASUAN: OK! We'll fight till the end. The battle of

14   *Armageddon*! Yes!

25. First Job

CAST: DAVID, JAMES
SETTING: The front porch of James' house

1 DAVID: Why do you look so depressed?
2 JAMES: I just got fired from my first job.
3 DAVID: Fired? Really?
4 JAMES: Yes. Axed. I was told I was finished. Never come back
5   again.
6 DAVID: Dang! How long did you work there?
7 JAMES: Forty-five minutes.
8 DAVID: Forty-five minutes? That's all?
9 JAMES: That's it! Hired and fired all under an hour.
10 DAVID: Wow. Guess you don't get a paycheck, huh?
11 JAMES: No! And the lady told me I owed her forty-seven
12   dollars!
13 DAVID: For what?
14 JAMES: Two new leashes for her dogs.
15 DAVID: Dog leashes? Where did you work?
16 JAMES: This lady who had two spoiled poodles hired me as
17   a dog walker. Peaches and Pebbles. Her precious
18   angels! And all I had to do was walk them in the park
19   for an hour each day and she'd pay me a hundred
20   dollars a week.
21 DAVID: Wow! Talk about easy money.
22 JAMES: That's what I thought. How hard can it be to walk
23   two stupid poodles in the park?
24 DAVID: Apparently harder than you thought. So what
25   happened?
26 JAMES: Let me paint the picture for you first. Peaches and
27   Pebbles are two white poodles. They are groomed to
28   perfection and they are not to get any dirt on them. Not
29   as much as a speck as Mrs. Worthington said.

1 DAVID: So you walk them in the grass ...

2 JAMES: Which is exactly what I was doing until this black

3   little prissy Maltese strutted by.

4 DAVID: Uh-oh.

5 JAMES: Then all of a sudden, Peaches and Pebbles started

6   running after this female. I wasn't ready for it and it

7   caught me off guard. They pulled on their leashes so

8   hard and I didn't have a tight grip on them and ...

9   *(Shakes head.)* There they went. Peaches and Pebbles

10   were running through the mud, barking and chasing

11   that stupid prissy Maltese ... It was horrible. They

12   were covered in mud from head to toe. Or rather

13   head to paw.

14 DAVID: But it wasn't your fault.

15 JAMES: I know. So anyway, I finally caught up with the

16   dirty little monsters and had a great idea. I gave them

17   a little bath in the duck pond. Washed all the mud off

18   of them before I took them home.

19 DAVID: Sounds good to me.

20 JAMES: Big mistake! Let me tell you, big mistake! First of

21   all, Peaches and Pebbles don't do baths. But ... they do

22   like to chase ducks. So there I am trying to wash the

23   mud off them and they take off across the pond,

24   chasing ducks. I'm screaming, "Come back here, you

25   dumb dogs!" But no. But who is coming? The park

26   manager, who shows me the sign ... "No pets in the

27   water."

28 DAVID: But it wasn't your fault.

29 JAMES: Exactly! Finally, I get them out of the pond after

30   they traipse through more mud so now not only do I

31   have mud-covered poodles, but stinky ones as well. So

32   now I'm holding onto their leashes really tight.

33   Surely I can find a water hose to rinse them off. But

34   then ...

35 DAVID: I don't know if I want to hear this.

1 JAMES: Peaches and Puddles see a squirrel.
2 DAVID: But you're holding onto the leashes this time,
3   right?
4 JAMES: I was ... until they got wrapped around and
5   around and around some bushes. I couldn't get them
6   untangled. And the only way to get the dogs back
7   home was to undo their leashes and carry them
8   home.
9 DAVID: So you carried home two stinky, muddy dogs
10   without their leashes? *(JAMES nods.)* No wonder you
11   got fired.
12 JAMES: But it wasn't my fault! Those dogs are horrible. I
13   bet I'm the hundredth dog walker Mrs. Worthington
14   has gone through.
15 DAVID: Well, maybe dog walking isn't your thing.
16 JAMES: That's what I'm thinking.
17 DAVID: There are other jobs out there.
18 JAMES: I know. I noticed an ad in the newspaper for a
19   babysitter for two little boys.
20 DAVID: You'd do that?
21 JAMES: Sure. For the money. How hard can it be to babysit
22   two three-year-old twins? Just tell them to play with
23   their toys while I watch TV. Easy money.
24 DAVID: You've never been around kids much, have you?
25 JAMES: Not really.
26 DAVID: I'll give you a day at it. No, half a day.
27 JAMES: You think I'll get fired from that job, too?
28 DAVID: Actually, I think you'll fire yourself.
29 JAMES: Why?
30 DAVID: Because of this. *(Cries and screams.)* "I want that
31   toy! He took my toy! I don't want to take a nap! I hate
32   naps! I don't want to play with my toys! I want that! I
33   want this! I don't want to! No! No! No!"
34 JAMES: It'd be like that?
35 DAVID: Yes. I'm afraid so.

1   JAMES: Dang! I think I'll look at being a lifeguard or
2   something like that.

3   DAVID: Good idea.

4   JAMES: I guess I'm just not good with animals or kids.

5   DAVID: You have to have a heart for them.

6   JAMES: Yeah. But I like snakes. Maybe I could be a snake
7   handler.

8   DAVID: That'd be the best job ever.

9   JAMES: I know. I should put my own ad in the paper.
10   "Experienced snake handler at your service."

11 DAVID: You should try that.

12 JAMES: I think I will.

26. Report Card

CAST: BLAKE, DANIEL
PROPS: Report card, pen, trash can
SETTING: School hallway

1 *(At rise, BLAKE is staring at his report card when DANIEL*
2 *enters.)*
3 **BLAKE: Holy moly!**
4 **DANIEL: Bad report card? I flunked PE. But I don't think**
5 **they'll make me go to summer school for PE, do you?**
6 **BLAKE:** *(Still looking at his report card)* **This can't be right.**
7 **DANIEL: That excuse probably won't work on your parents.**
8 **Schools don't normally make mistakes when it comes**
9 **to issuing report cards. Take my forty-three in PE for**
10 **example, I earned it. And that's what they put on the**
11 **card. A big fat forty-three.**
12 **BLAKE: How do you flunk PE?**
13 **DANIEL: Not suiting out cost me most of the failing grade.**
14 **I'd always forget and leave my gym clothes at home.**
15 **Plus, I'm clumsy. Don't ask me to run the obstacle**
16 **course without falling down, getting stuck on the**
17 **parallel bars, and knocking over the hurdles. They**
18 **can't send me to summer school for failing PE, can**
19 **they?**
20 **BLAKE: I don't know.** *(Looks back at report card.)*
21 **Unbelievable!**
22 **DANIEL: Bet you'll be going, won't you?**
23 **BLAKE: Where?**
24 **DANIEL: Summer school.**
25 **BLAKE: Me? Why?**
26 **DANIEL: Obviously your report card stinks.**
27 **BLAKE: No. Quite the opposite. Straight As.** *(Shows DANIEL*
28 *the report card.)*

1   DANIEL: Holy moly! How did you do that?

2   BLAKE: I don't know.

3   DANIEL: Do you think the school messed up? A computer
4   glitch?

5   BLAKE: I hope not.

6   DANIEL: Well, if they did, we won't tell anyone, will we?
7   Dang. I wish they'd messed up and made my forty-
8   three in PE a ninety-three. *(Takes out a pen.)* But
9   maybe with a little artwork ... *(Marks on his report*
10   *card.)*

11   BLAKE: You're going to change your grade?

12   DANIEL: With a little curve right there. I believe ... yes ... I
13   just turned this forty-three into a ninety-three.
14   Perfecto! Look.

15   BLAKE: Daniel, that is so obvious. Your parents will know
16   what you did.

17   DANIEL: I think I'll take my chances. *(Waves report card.)*
18   See Mom ... see Dad ... As and Cs in all my classes.

19   BLAKE: You mean, all Cs except for the one F in PE.

20   DANIEL: Nope. A in PE!

21   BLAKE: Liar.

22   DANIEL: Look who's talking. You're holding onto a
23   computer-glitched report card and you're planning to
24   show it to your parents.

25   BLAKE: *(Waves report card.)* This was all my hard work.

26   DANIEL: Sure, sure.

27   BLAKE: It's true! My parents grounded me over my last
28   report card. Which meant no TV, no computer, no
29   hanging out with friends ... nothing! And they also cut
30   me off from being able to send or receive text
31   messages. My phone was for emergencies only or for
32   my parents to check up on me. So in essence, my life
33   was school and homework. Period.

34   DANIEL: That's terrible.

35   BLAKE: It was, but ... *(Looks at report card.)* But it paid off.

1   **Straight As.**

2   **DANIEL: So does this mean you're no longer grounded?**

3   **BLAKE: I think so.**

4   **DANIEL: Back to civilization for you then. You can go back**
5   **to sending out a thousand or so text messages a day,**
6   **social networking, gaming ...**

7   **BLAKE: Yeah, but I think I'll try to keep this up.**

8   **DANIEL: The good grades?**

9   **BLAKE: Yeah. I'm actually proud of myself.** *(Pats himself.)*
10   **I think I'll just pat myself on the back.**

11 **DANIEL:** *(Looks at report card.)* **And I'm proud of this. I**
12   **think my forty-three looks like a ninety-three, don't**
13   **you?**

14 **BLAKE: No. I think it looks like you changed it.**

15 **DANIEL: I'll be fast.** *(Waves report card.)* **See, Mom! See,**
16   **Dad! All Cs and one A. Nothing to ground me for here.**

17 **BLAKE: Seriously Daniel, who makes a forty-three in PE?**

18 **DANIEL: Not me. I made a ninety-three!**

19 **BLAKE:** *(Shakes head.)* **You're going to get caught. But hey,**
20   **if you do, then you can have no social life like me and**
21   **maybe the next time around you'll make all As.**

22 **DANIEL: I doubt it. I'm bad in PE.** *(As they exit)* **Wanna see**
23   **me jump over that trash can?** *(Jumps over it, but*
24   *knocks it down and falls.)* **See, I'm bad.**

25 **BLAKE: Maybe they will send you to summer school for**
26   **PE.**

27 **DANIEL:** *(Standing up)* **You think?**

28 **BLAKE: Maybe.**

29 **DANIEL: Man!**

27. Double Dare

CAST: CODY, JOHN
SETTING: School hallway

1   CODY: I double dare you.

2   JOHN: Why are you doing this to me? You know I can't say no

3   to a dare. And a double dare ... Dang!

4   CODY: I know. Remember last week when I dared you to

5   stand on Mrs. Castillo's desk and jump across four

6   desks?

7   JOHN: And I made it!

8   CODY: Not before Mrs. Castillo walked in the room.

9   JOHN: I know. I'd jumped off the desk just as she walked in.

10 CODY: "John, what do you think you are doing?" At least you

11   were honest.

12 JOHN: "Taking a dare, Mrs. Castillo."

13 CODY: And she said, "John, if I dared you to jump off the

14   roof of this building, would you do that?"

15 JOHN: "Yes, ma'am."

16 CODY: *(Points.)* "To the office now!"

17 JOHN: And I got into trouble didn't I, Cody? So stop daring

18   me to do stuff. Mr. Sikes doesn't want to see my face

19   again.

20 CODY: But John, this dare won't get you sent to the office.

21 JOHN: I wouldn't count on that.

22 CODY: I'm only daring you to do something you already

23   want to do, but you just don't have the courage to do it

24   on your own.

25 JOHN: You're right about that.

26 CODY: So I double dare you to ask Emily on a date.

27 JOHN: Come on, Cody, dare me to do something else.

28   Anything else. Like put a mouse in a teacher's drawer.

29 CODY: You did that last month.

1   JOHN: Or dare me to try out for a school play and I'll be as
2   bad as possible. Or good. Whichever you dare me to
3   do.
4   CODY: You already did that one, too.
5   JOHN: Yeah, and it was easy since I'm so terrible at acting.
6   I humiliated myself in front of everyone on that dare.
7   Because you know, I take dares very seriously. I will
8   conquer them! I have no fear. I'll jump across desks,
9   off the roof of the building, you name it, but what
10   you're asking me to do ...
11   CODY: And it's a double dare at that.
12   JOHN: Cody, why are you doing this to me?
13   CODY: Because you and I both know you like Emily. And
14   it's the only way you'll ever ask her out.
15   JOHN: But I can't! What if she says no?
16   CODY: What if she says yes?
17   JOHN: Dare me to do something else. Please! How about
18   streak through the cafeteria?
19   CODY: You already did that. Well, in your swimming
20   trunks.
21   JOHN: Swipe some hall passes?
22   CODY: John, you did that, too. I have enough hall passes to
23   last me until my senior year.
24   JOHN: Sing a song over the school intercom?
25   CODY: That's so old. You did that twice already. And you
26   actually sounded pretty good, which took most of the
27   fun out of it. You should be in choir.
28   JOHN: Then think of something new. Double dare it if you
29   want to. I'm ready. Give it to me!
30   CODY: I dare you to ask Emily out. I double dare you.
31   JOHN: No!
32   CODY: You're actually turning down a dare? A double dare
33   at that?
34   JOHN: Cody, you're killing me.
35   CODY: I double dare you, John.

1   JOHN: All right! All right, I'll do it.

2   CODY: You will?

3   JOHN: Yes.

4   CODY: When?

5   JOHN: During math class.

6   CODY: Today?

7   JOHN: Yes, today.

8   CODY: Perfect. I'll be there to witness your actions.

9   JOHN: I can't believe I'm going to do this.

10 CODY: And what if Emily says yes?

11 JOHN: I'll be the happiest guy alive in the entire world.

12   And I'll thank you for the rest of my life for daring me

13   to do it.

14 CODY: And what if she says no?

15 JOHN: I'll look at her and shrug and say, "It's OK. It was

16   just a dare anyway. I didn't want you to say yes,

17   anyways."

18 CODY: Liar.

19 JOHN: You know what, Cody?

20 CODY: What?

21 JOHN: After this stunt, I dare you, no double dare you, not

22   to dare me anything again.

23 CODY: You pull this off and you've got it.

24 JOHN: Thanks. Hey, do you think Emily will say yes?

25 CODY: I do.

26 JOHN: Why's that?

27 CODY: *(Smiles.)* Because she's the one who asked me to

28   dare you to ask her out.

29 JOHN: What? Really?

30 CODY: Really. Sorry, dude. You've got this dare all

31   wrapped up. I was just having fun giving you a hard

32   time.

33 JOHN: Wow! I can't believe it. Yes!

34 CODY: Hey, I have another one for you ...

35 JOHN: Hey, you promised no more dares if I pulled this

1   one off.

2   CODY: You haven't yet. So, I dare you to stand on the table

3   and sing "I'm a Little Teapot" in the cafeteria during

4   lunch. No, I double dare you!

5   JOHN: Ah, man! You know I can't say no.

6   CODY: I know, and this is going to be great.

7   JOHN: *(As they exit, he sings.)* "I'm a little teapot, short and

8   stout, here is my handle and here is my spout. When

9   I get all steamed up, hear me shout, tip me over and

10   pour me out."

28. Creepy Crawly

CAST: MR. SIKES, ANDREW
PROPS: Book, broom
SETTING: Classroom

1   *(At rise, ANDREW sits at his desk, staring at the ceiling.*
2   *There is an empty desk next to his. After a moment, MR.*
3   *SIKES notices him.)*
4   **MR. SIKES: May I ask what you're doing?**
5   **ANDREW:** *(Points to the ceiling.)* **Look.**
6   **MR. SIKES: Andrew, you need to be looking at your textbook**
7   **and reading chapter twelve.**
8   **ANDREW: But there's a huge spider on the ceiling and it's**
9   **right above my head.**
10   **MR. SIKES: Well, you ignore the spider and he'll ignore you.**
11   **ANDREW: But what if he falls on me?**
12   **MR. SIKES: He won't.**
13   **ANDREW: I'm sorry, Mr. Sikes, but I'm creeped out knowing**
14   **he's up there.**
15   **MR. SIKES: And I'm creeped out knowing you're not**
16   **following my instructions. Which is to read chapter**
17   **twelve.**
18   **ANDREW: But ...** *(Points.)* **It's huge.**
19   **MR. SIKES: May I ask, how did you even know that the**
20   **spider was on the ceiling when you were supposed to**
21   **be reading?**
22   **ANDREW: Well, I was feeling a little stiff so I stretched like**
23   **this ...** *(Demonstrates, looking up when he stretches.)* **And**
24   **that's when I saw him. I think he's lost.**
25   **MR. SIKES: I think you'll be lost when we have a chapter**
26   **review test in the morning.**
27   **ANDREW: We could get a broom.**
28   **MR. SIKES: For what?**

1 ANDREW: Then I could stand on my desk and get him to
2   crawl on the broom, then run over to the window
3   and set him free.
4 MR. SIKES: Andrew, ignore the spider and read.
5 ANDREW: I bet he crawled up there looking for a way
6   outside.
7 MR. SIKES: You don't know that.
8 ANDREW: Mr. Sikes, he's probably hungry and thirsty. As
9   a matter of fact, I am too. I'm glad lunch is next
10   period.
11 MR. SIKES: Ignore the spider.
12 ANDREW: It's hard ignoring him knowing he's there. You
13   know? I mean, I don't like spiders in the first place
14   and they do creep me out. But I also feel sorry for
15   him if that makes any sense. Do you like spiders, Mr.
16   Sikes?
17 MR. SIKES: No. Do you like the principal's office?
18 ANDREW: No, but it's not like it's my fault there's possibly
19   a killer spider hanging above my head. It's not
20   exactly a safe environment if you ask me.
21 MR. SIKES: Ignore the spider and read! Please.
22 ANDREW: I'll try.
23 MR. SIKES: Thank you.
24 ANDREW: *(Reads for a moment, then looks up.)* Mr. Sikes,
25   he's kind of dangling now. I think he's going to fall on
26   my head and bite me. And what if it's a recluse? Then
27   while I'm on my deathbed I'll have to tell them ... you
28   know, the media ... that I begged you to let me change
29   seats and you said no.
30 MR. SIKES: When did you beg me to let you change seats?
31 ANDREW: Now.
32 MR. SIKES: Then move.
33 ANDREW: *(Moves to the empty desk next to him.)* Thank
34   you.
35 MR. SIKES: Now read.

1 **ANDREW:** *(Reads for a moment, then looks up.)* **Oh, great!**

2 **MR. SIKES: What now?**

3 **ANDREW: He followed me over here.**

4 **MR. SIKES: What are you talking about?**

5 **ANDREW: He must like me. Look!** *(Points to the ceiling.)*

6 **MR. SIKES:** *(Looks up.)* **Well, I'll be ...**

7 **ANDREW: Can I change seats again?**

8 **MR. SIKES: Change! Just change! Then go back to your**

9 **reading.**

10 **ANDREW:** *(Changes seats, reads for a moment, then looks*

11 *up.)* **Mr. Sikes ...**

12 **MR. SIKES: What?**

13 **ANDREW: He did it again.**

14 **MR. SIKES: Again?**

15 **ANDREW: He must think I'm his mommy. Well, daddy.**

16 **Can I change seats again?**

17 **MR. SIKES: No!**

18 **ANDREW: But —**

19 **MR. SIKES:** *(Hands him a broom.)* **Kill him!**

20 **ANDREW:** *(Takes the broom.)* **I'm not going to kill him! I'm**

21 **going to set him free.** *(Stands on his desk with the*

22 *broom.)* **Come here, little spider. Come on. Get on the**

23 **broom, and I'll let you go outside. Come on ... Oh, no!**

24 *(Looks down on the floor.)* **He fell.**

25 **MR. SIKES:** *(Stomps his foot on the ground.)* **Problem solved!**

26 **ANDREW: Mr. Sikes, you killed him!**

27 **MR. SIKES: Yes. Now read chapter twelve.**

28 **ANDREW: You didn't have to kill him. I was going to let**

29 **him go outside.**

30 **MR. SIKES: Well, it's over now and you need to read. So**

31 **read!** *(ANDREW sits down and tries to read. He starts to*

32 *cry.)* **You're crying? Over a spider?**

33 **ANDREW: He thought I was his mommy. Or daddy, that is.**

34 *(Looks up at the ceiling.)* **And now I kind of miss him.**

35 **MR. SIKES:** *Read!*

29. Humongous Crush

CAST: NOAH, PAUL
PROPS: Cell phone
SETTING: School hallway

1   NOAH: Paul, guess what I heard.
2   PAUL: What? What? Was it another rumor about me? What is
3   it this time? I shave my legs? No, that was last week. My
4   family lives in a bus? No, that was last month.
5   Hmmmm ... Let me guess ... *(Suddenly)* I have a
6   humongous crush on Miss Robinson. Well, actually,
7   that's true. So if that's what you heard ... well, it's a fact,
8   not fiction.
9   NOAH: You have a crush on Miss Robinson?
10 PAUL: Major crush. I want to marry her. But I'm sure that
11   even if she did fall in love with me, it'd be against
12   school policy for her to date me. Wouldn't it?
13 NOAH: Well, duh.
14 PAUL: But maybe we could have lunch together.
15 NOAH: Where? In the cafeteria?
16 PAUL: Why not?
17 NOAH: She wouldn't do that. What would the other teachers
18   say? The students? And what are you going to do? Go
19   through the cafeteria line together and offer to buy her
20   lunch? Tell the cafeteria lady to punch your ticket twice?
21 PAUL: I don't know. It was just an idea. Maybe we could go
22   into the teachers' lounge.
23 NOAH: You can't go in there. Students aren't allowed.
24 PAUL: Well, if she invited me ...
25 NOAH: She's not going to do that.
26 PAUL: You never know. Look! There she is. *(Waves.)* Hi Elaine!
27 NOAH: You call Miss Robinson by her first name? Elaine?
28 PAUL: Look! She smiled and waved at me. I think she

113

1   winked, too.

2 NOAH: Again, you call Miss Robinson by her first name?

3 PAUL: I've just started that. I want her to think of me as

4   her equal.

5 NOAH: You're a student, Paul.

6 PAUL: Did you see her wink at me?

7 NOAH: No.

8 PAUL: I did. If she'll just wait for me to graduate from

9   school, then we can start dating.

10 NOAH: Are you serious?

11 PAUL: I think I'll write her a letter tonight.

12 NOAH: Who writes letters?

13 PAUL: Well, I can't text her because I don't know her

14   phone number. I don't have her personal e-mail

15   address either. And besides, a letter would seem more

16   ... you know ... romantic. Don't you think?

17 NOAH: I think a text can be romantic. But I would never,

18   in a million years, text my teacher.

19 PAUL: I'll say, "Dearest Elaine ... "

20 NOAH: Dearest?

21 PAUL: "My love ... "

22 NOAH: Oh, brother!

23 PAUL: "I must confess my feelings for you before I explode.

24   Oh, Elaine ... I so love you! And I realize the age

25   difference and the fact that you're my teacher and it's

26   against school policy to date ... but Elaine, my love ... if

27   you could just wait for me to graduate. Yes, wait a few

28   years then we can see each other and show the world

29   a love that will last forever!"

30 NOAH: Paul!

31 PAUL: *(Still dreamy eyes)* Yes?

32 NOAH: Don't do it.

33 PAUL: But I love her.

34 NOAH: Paul, if you've ever listened to any advice I've given

35   to you, now is the time.

1 PAUL: I'll write her the perfect love letter tonight, then in
2   the morning, I'll slip it in her hand. I bet she'll give
3   my hand a tight squeeze as she takes the letter. Then
4   she'll probably wink at me again.
5 NOAH: No, she'll think it's a note from your parents.
6 PAUL: Maybe I'll give her a rose with the letter. Yes. A
7   single rose. That's romantic!
8 NOAH: You're going to be sent to the principal's office
9   over this.
10 PAUL: For giving Elaine a rose?
11 NOAH: For flirting with Miss Robinson!
12 PAUL: No I won't. I bet by sixth period she'll hand me a
13   note asking me for my phone number. And then I can
14   call her and we can make plans ...
15 NOAH: Plans for what?
16 PAUL: To stay true to each other until I graduate from
17   school.
18 NOAH: So you won't be dating anyone else?
19 PAUL: Absolutely not.
20 NOAH: Then I'll let Rachel know —
21 PAUL: Let Rachel know what?
22 NOAH: That you're not interested in her. Because I heard
23   she wants to go out with you. But if you're tied down
24   to Miss Robinson ...
25 PAUL: Really? Rachel wants to go out with me?
26 NOAH: That's what I heard.
27 PAUL: Seriously?
28 NOAH: I swear.
29 PAUL: *(Not believing this)* Rachel wants to date me?
30 NOAH: She told Bobby she liked you and wanted him to
31   get me to ask you if you were interested too, and if
32   you were interested, Bobby or I would text her back
33   and let her know. But if you're not, I'll text her a big
34   fat no.
35 PAUL: No!

1 **NOAH: No?**

2 **PAUL: No, don't text her. I mean, don't text her "no." Text**

3   **her "yes." I'll go out with her.**

4 **NOAH: You will?**

5 **PAUL: Yes!**

6 **NOAH: But what about Miss Robinson?**

7 **PAUL: Elaine will just have to find someone her own age.**

8   **Rachel is like so hot ... Wow! I can't believe she likes**

9   **me.**

10 **NOAH: So you want me to text Rachel and let her know**

11   **you're interested?**

12 **PAUL: Yes! Oh, yes!**

13 **NOAH: And Miss Robinson?**

14 **PAUL: I'm over her. And thanks for the advice, Noah. I**

15   **know Miss Robinson would've fallen head over heels**

16   **in love with me, but I'm too young to put my life on**

17   **hold for her. If she wants to wait on me, well, that's**

18   **fine. Heck, I bet she starts winking at me again in**

19   **sixth period. I'll just have to let her down easily.**

20 **NOAH: You can do it, Paul.**

21 **PAUL: I'll try. Hey, will you text Rachel now?**

22 **NOAH: Sure.**

23 **PAUL: And tell her to text me.**

24 **NOAH: OK.**

25 **PAUL: And tell her we were meant to be together.**

26 **NOAH: So soon?**

27 **PAUL: Yes. Rachel is the girl of my dreams.**

28 **NOAH: Dude, you've got to slow down.**

29 **PAUL: You know what I'm going to tell her when she texts**

30   **me?**

31 **NOAH: What?**

32 **PAUL: "Rachel, I love you! I've loved you from afar for so**

33   **long." Do you think I should write her a letter? I think**

34   **I should. It's romantic. And I'll get her a rose. A single**

35   **rose. Oh, Rachel, I love you!** *(NOAH shakes his head.)*

30. One-Way

CAST: LUKE, JUAN
PROPS: Cell phones, food for eating in the car
SETTING: Car

1 (*At rise, LUKE is sitting in the driver's seat of a car talking*
2 *to JUAN, who is in the passenger's seat. As LUKE is driving*
3 *and talking, he is also eating and texting.*)
4 LUKE: And then Amber said, "I'll go out with you Luke if
5   your friend Juan comes along and goes out with Amy."
6 JUAN: No way.
7 LUKE: Yes way. I'm texting her right now and telling her
8   you'd love to.
9 JUAN: You bet! Amy is ... wow ... she's just wow!
10 LUKE: I'm thinking we'll grab a bite to eat then catch a
11   movie. Maybe even a chick flick if that's what the girls
12   want to do.
13 JUAN: And afterwards maybe we could take them for a drive
14   through the park.
15 LUKE: And we can park then walk down to the duck pond.
16   Girls like that. They think it's romantic or something.
17 JUAN: (*Smiles.*) Yeah, then ... (*Makes a kissing sound. Glances*
18   *up, then screams.*)
19 LUKE: What? (*Glances up from his cell phone and also*
20   *screams as he slams on the brakes.*)
21 JUAN: (*Covering his face*) Are we dead?
22 LUKE: No! I pulled over.
23 JUAN: (*Peeks through his hands.*) Are you sure we're not dead?
24 LUKE: We're still alive.
25 JUAN: Luke, you almost killed us. You just drove down a one-
26   way street. Going the wrong way! All the cars were
27   coming this way, and we were going that way.
28 LUKE: (*Holds out his hand to show JUAN.*) My hands are still

1   shaking.

2   JUAN: And my heart is pounding!

3   LUKE: What do I do now?

4   JUAN: Turn around! We're going the wrong way on a one-
5   way street.

6   LUKE: But look at all the cars coming this way.

7   JUAN: And thank goodness you pulled over in the nick of time.

8   LUKE: Man, that was scary.

9   JUAN: I was scared! I thought my life was about to end.
10   Sixteen years old. A life cut short. I didn't get to
11   graduate, get married, have kids ... and worst of all, go
12   on that date with Amy.

13   LUKE: Juan, I don't know what to do.

14   JUAN: Turn around.

15   LUKE: I'm scared to turn around. Heck, I'm scared to
16   drive now. We did almost die.

17   JUAN: Well, I can't drive. I don't have my permit yet.

18   LUKE: *(Drops head.)* Juan, I almost killed you.

19   JUAN: Yes, you did. And didn't they tell you in drivers ed
20   not to text and drive or eat and drive and to pay
21   attention to the road?

22   LUKE: I thought I was paying attention.

23   JUAN: Obviously not. I don't think you're supposed to
24   multitask while driving. And I haven't even taken
25   drivers ed yet.

26   LUKE: You're not. I'm an idiot.

27   JUAN: Well ... live and learn.

28   LUKE: I could have died at the young age of sixteen.

29   JUAN: Me, too! One minute we're planning our dates with
30   Amber and Amy, and the next our bloody bodies are
31   sprawled out on the pavement and we're looking
32   down at them. Thinking ... this is weird. Am I dead?

33   LUKE: Juan, what are you talking about?

34   JUAN: You know. That out-of-body experience when you
35   die and you're suddenly looking around wondering

1   why your body is over there and you're up here

2   looking at it. Then I guess we'll just float on up ...

3   LUKE: I'd probably sink down there. If you know what I

4   mean.

5   JUAN: Hell?

6   LUKE: *(Cries.)* Yes! For killing us!

7   JUAN: It would've been an accident.

8   LUKE: But I knew better. I learned it in drivers ed class.

9   And my mom and dad are constantly reminding me

10   ... don't text and drive!

11   JUAN: And you were eating, too.

12   LUKE: And look what happened!

13   JUAN: We almost had a head-on collision.

14   LUKE: Juan, I'm so sorry!

15   JUAN: I forgive you, Luke. But can we turn this vehicle

16   around and head the right direction? Facing the

17   wrong direction on a one-way street is really freaking

18   me out ... even if we're not moving.

19   LUKE: Yeah. OK. Here, you hold onto my phone.

20   JUAN: And no eating. Keep your eyes on the road and your

21   hands on the steering wheel.

22   LUKE: I will! From now on, that's exactly what I'm going

23   to do.

24   JUAN: And while you safely get us home, I will text Amber

25   for you. *(Texts.)* Juan would love to go out with Amy.

26   It's a date!

27   LUKE: *(Driving)* Going the right direction now. Slow and

28   steady. Keeping my eyes on the road and my hands

29   on the steering wheel from now on.

30   JUAN: *(Takes a deep breath.)* I'm glad we're not dead.

31   LUKE: Me too.

32   JUAN: Now back to us taking the girls to the duck pond.

33   They think it's romantic?

34   LUKE: That's what I've heard.

35   JUAN: Perfect. *(Puckers up and makes kissing sounds.)*

31. Last Man Standing

CAST: JIMAR, BRYAN
SETTING: Hallway

1 JIMAR: So in PE today, we got to pick teams. And guess who
2   got picked last?
3 BRYAN: You picked teams?
4 JIMAR: Yeah, Coach Lewis said we had to.
5 BRYAN: But that's so sixth grade.
6 JIMAR: It felt like sixth grade. Because you're standing there
7   thinking, "Please, please, someone pick me. Don't let
8   me be the last one standing." And guess what?
9 BRYAN: You were the last one standing?
10 JIMAR: Yep. And when Tony saw he had to choose between
11   me and Eugene, he picked Eugene. I was thinking,
12   "Seriously, dude? Eugene has two left feet and wears
13   thick glasses and everyone knows he's the worst athlete
14   in school." But Tony looked at Eugene and picked him.
15   Then Hunter, the team captain for the other team,
16   looked at me and said, "Guess I'm stuck with you." I
17   was like, "Really? Am I that bad?"
18 BRYAN: So what were they choosing sides for? Baseball?
19 JIMAR: Dodgeball.
20 BRYAN: Seriously?
21 JIMAR: Seriously.
22 BRYAN: Talk about being sixth grade! I haven't played that
23   since I was twelve.
24 JIMAR: Me too! OK, so you know the last person standing
25   without getting hit by the ball wins the game for their
26   team?
27 BRYAN: Yeah, I remember that. So how'd it go?
28 JIMAR: You are looking at the last man standing.
29 BRYAN: You won the game for your team?

1   JIMAR: That's right. I was the last man chosen, but I was
2   the last man standing. Yes, I won it for the team who
3   didn't even want me in the first place.
4   BRYAN: Way to go, Jimar! *(They high-five.)*
5   JIMAR: And you should've seen me! Those balls were
6   being thrown at my back, at my feet, my head …
7   BRYAN: But I thought in dodgeball you were only
8   supposed to hit from the waist down.
9   JIMAR: Yeah, in elementary. But in high school, all bets
10   are off. I saw a couple of kids get hit pretty hard in
11   the head.
12 BRYAN: And Coach Lewis didn't say anything about it?
13 JIMAR: Sure, he said, "Well, you should've been watching.
14   You're out! O-u-t! Out!"
15 BRYAN: Dang!
16 JIMAR: So after being the last person picked, I was
17   determined to be the last man standing. I was like
18   this. *(Demonstrates moving around, jumping, ducking,*
19   *throwing, etc.)* That ball wasn't going to hit me.
20 BRYAN: Man, you are quick.
21 JIMAR: And when it was down to me and Sid from the
22   other side, my team was cheering me on. "Come on,
23   Jimar! You can do it! Jimar! Jimar! Jimar!" Suddenly I
24   went from loser boy to being the team's only hope.
25   And when Sid threw the ball my way, I did this …
26   *(Demonstrates by screaming, then jumping in the air.)*
27 BRYAN: That's awesome!
28 JIMAR: Then I got the ball, looked across the gym, and
29   gave Sid my evil eye. Like this. *(Demonstrates.)* Now it
30   was my chance to win it all. I'd show them they
31   should be sorry for picking me last. Then I was like
32   this … *(As if throwing the ball)* Kabam! Yes! I got him!
33   Smack between the eyes. He fell over and I was
34   suddenly being circled by my teammates. "Jimar!
35   Jimar! Jimar!" They even picked me up and held me

1   in the air. "Jimar! Jimar! Jimar!"

2   BRYAN: Man, that's great! That's the way to win the game.

3   JIMAR: Guess who gets to be the team captain tomorrow?

4   BRYAN: You do?

5   JIMAR: That's right. Me! Because I can do this better than

6   anyone else. *(Demonstrates by jumping, kicking, and*

7   *moving around fast.)*

8   BRYAN: So the moral of your story is ... you can be chosen

9   last, but it doesn't mean you have to be last.

10   JIMAR: That's right! *(Holding up his hands)* Winner, here!

11   Winner! Thank you! Thank you! Jimar is my name

12   and dodgeball is my game.

13   BRYAN: That's great, but you know ... dodgeball in high

14   school ... ?

15   JIMAR: I know. It's so sixth grade. But oh well. I get to be

16   the team captain tomorrow. Yes!

32. Personal Responsibility

CAST: MR. YOUNG, ANTHONY
PROPS: Grade book, test papers, history book
SETTING: Classroom

1   *(At rise, ANTHONY is standing at MR. YOUNG's desk.)*
2   MR. YOUNG: Anthony, let's talk about your grades.
3   ANTHONY: *(Quickly)* **Did you call my parents?**
4   MR. YOUNG: Not yet.
5   ANTHONY: Are you going to?
6   MR. YOUNG: I thought I'd send your parents an e-mail.
7   Report cards don't go out for three more weeks, and I
8   think they should know what's going on.
9   ANTHONY: Mr. Young, can we talk about this first? See, my
10   parents don't really like to get involved in my business.
11 MR. YOUNG: Excuse me?
12 ANTHONY: It's called personal responsibility. They expect
13   me to deal with my failures on my own. Sort of like that
14   Vegas saying.
15 MR. YOUNG: What Vegas saying?
16 ANTHONY: What happens in Vegas stays in Vegas.
17 MR. YOUNG: This isn't Vegas.
18 ANTHONY: No, no, it's like that saying. So, what happens in
19   school stays in school. That's how my parents feel.
20 MR. YOUNG: Are you serious?
21 ANTHONY: Serious as a heart attack.
22 MR. YOUNG: That's not funny. My father died from a heart
23   attack.
24 ANTHONY: Oh, I'm sorry ... sir. But you have to understand
25   that my parents are busy people. If they even take the
26   time to look at your e-mail they will say, "Son, it's up to
27   you to fix this." So that's what I'm going to do. Fix this.
28   Mr. Young, how can I fix this?

1 MR. YOUNG: Anthony, your average in my class is a thirty-
2   eight.
3 ANTHONY: Thirty-eight? How did that happen?
4 MR. YOUNG: I'll be happy to tell you. *(Opens his grade*
5   *book.)* Failure to turn in eight out of twelve
6   assignments. You made a fifty-three on the last test
7   and a sixty-seven on the one before that. Pop quiz
8   grades ... zero, zero, zero, and zero.
9 ANTHONY: Mr. Young ...
10 MR. YOUNG: Yes, Anthony?
11 ANTHONY: American history is difficult for me.
12 MR. YOUNG: Have you thought about studying?
13 ANTHONY: Which is what I plan to start doing! Studying
14   every single night. Every night and every day.
15 MR. YOUNG: That will be a good start. Let's see how you
16   did on today's pop quiz. *(Shuffles through several*
17   *papers.)* Uh-huh ... as I expected. *(Looks at ANTHONY.)*
18   Zero. Can you believe that?
19 ANTHONY: Darn! And I tried so hard.
20 MR. YOUNG: You tried hard? You didn't even answer the
21   question. The page is blank.
22 ANTHONY: But I tried so hard to remember the answer.
23 MR. YOUNG: *(Writing in the grade book)* Another zero.
24   That's going to bring your grade down even further.
25 ANTHONY: But tonight, I'm taking my history book home
26   and reading it from cover to cover.
27 MR. YOUNG: Why don't you start by reading chapter
28   twenty-three? Where we're at this week?
29 ANTHONY: I will, but I have one little problem. I lost my
30   book. Can you believe that?
31 MR. YOUNG: *(As if he is shocked)* No!
32 ANTHONY: It's true. And that's why I have a thirty-eight in
33   history.
34 MR. YOUNG: So you're telling me that all you need is a new
35   book and the problem will be solved?

1   **ANTHONY:** Yes sir.

2   **MR. YOUNG:** Anthony, have you looked in your locker?

3   **ANTHONY:** Well, I ...

4   **MR. YOUNG:** I did.

5   **ANTHONY:** You looked in my locker? Isn't that like
6   trespassing? Isn't there privacy laws concerning
7   snooping around in students' lockers?

8   **MR. YOUNG:** *(Hands him a book.)* **Here you go. Your book.**

9   **ANTHONY:** Well, what do you know! It was hiding in my
10   locker.

11   **MR. YOUNG:** Now read it.

12   **ANTHONY:** Yeah, yeah, I'm going to. It sure is a thick
13   book, isn't it? *(Opens book.)* With big words, too. Wow!
14   This is going to take me forever to read.

15   **MR. YOUNG:** And as a reminder, we're having a chapter
16   test tomorrow.

17   **ANTHONY:** Oh, OK. What chapter was that?

18   **MR. YOUNG:** Chapter twenty-three. Do you ever pay
19   attention in my class?

20   **ANTHONY:** Yeah, but see ... Jade sits up and over one row
21   from me and ... Mr. Young ... she's so pretty!

22   **MR. YOUNG:** So we have a little distraction, do we?

23   **ANTHONY:** *(Smiling)* Brown hair, blue eyes ... that cute
24   little smile ... And sometimes Jade turns around and
25   smiles at me. And when she does that ... *Wow!*

26   **MR. YOUNG:** And you lose all your concentration?

27   **ANTHONY:** Exactly!

28   **MR. YOUNG:** Well, tomorrow morning ... you ... front row.

29   **ANTHONY:** What?

30   **MR. YOUNG:** You'll start sitting in the front row
31   tomorrow.

32   **ANTHONY:** But I don't like sitting in the front row.

33   **MR. YOUNG:** Not my problem.

34   **ANTHONY:** But —

35   **MR. YOUNG:** And you better ace the chapter twenty-three

1   test tomorrow morning ... or else.

2 ANTHONY: Or else?

3 MR. YOUNG: Let me just say this: What happens in my

4   history class, stays in my history class. *(Makes a*

5   *cutting-throat gesture.)* If you know what I mean. OK,

6   off you go. Study, study, study!

7 ANTHONY: Uh, Mr. Young?

8 MR. YOUNG: Yes?

9 ANTHONY: Are you still e-mailing my parents?

10 MR. YOUNG: *(Smiles.)* Anthony, you were wrong.

11 ANTHONY: About what?

12 MR. YOUNG: Your parents do care about you.

13 ANTHONY: They do?

14 MR. YOUNG: Yes. I've already e-mailed them and heard

15   back from them.

16 ANTHONY: You have?

17 MR. YOUNG: *(Smiles.)* I have one word for you. *(Cheerfully)*

18   Grounded!

19 ANTHONY: Ah, man!

20 MR. YOUNG: Off you go now. Have fun! Study, study,

21   study! And remember, tomorrow, front row for you.

33. The Proposal

CAST: RYAN, COREY
SETTING: Outside of school as lunch has just begun

1   **RYAN:** *(Pointing)* **She's the one. That's her. Right there.**

2   **COREY: When are you going to tell her?**

3   **RYAN: I'm working on it.**

4   **COREY: Why don't you bump into her between classes and**

5   **say, "One of these days you're going to marry me."**

6   **RYAN: I'm not going to be that straightforward. I need to**

7   **ease into this.**

8   **COREY: How do you plan to do that?**

9   **RYAN: First, I'm going to ask her to go to a movie with me.**

10 **COREY: That's a good start. Especially since you don't even**

11   **know if you two like each other or not.**

12 **RYAN: Oh, I more than like her. I love her!**

13 **COREY: Ryan, you can't love her. You don't even know her.**

14 **RYAN: Corey, haven't you ever heard of love at first sight?**

15 **COREY: Is that what happened?**

16 **RYAN: First day of school ... Mrs. Otter's class ... that's when**

17   **I knew. I was in love with Nicole and I was going to**

18   **marry her.**

19 **COREY: Do you two have a class together?**

20 **RYAN: Fourth period. Economics.**

21 **COREY: Do you sit by each other?**

22 **RYAN: No.**

23 **COREY: Text?**

24 **RYAN: Not yet.**

25 **COREY: Smile at each other from across the room?**

26 **RYAN: Oh, I smile at her, but she hasn't noticed me yet.**

27 **COREY: Uh-huh.**

28 **RYAN: Uh-huh, what?**

29 **COREY: Ryan, you're living in a fantasy world and when**

1   your future wife refuses to acknowledge you, go on a
2   date with you, or for that matter, give you her phone
3   number ... *(Shakes head and pats RYAN on the back.)*
4   I'll be here for you my friend.
5 RYAN: Some friend you are. You have no faith. That girl is
6   going to fall hard for me. That is, when she notices
7   me.
8 COREY: She seems to have her eyes on that guy getting
9   into that black Mustang. Do you think she has a
10   boyfriend?
11 RYAN: I don't know. I don't think so.
12 COREY: Think she cares that you drive a 96 Ford Taurus
13   with a few dents here and there?
14 RYAN: It gets me around.
15 COREY: Do you think she knows your name?
16 RYAN: I'm sure she does because Mrs. Otter is always
17   calling on me. Especially when I'm not paying
18   attention. Then she yells at me. "Ryan! Are you even
19   listening to me?" Then I look away from my beautiful
20   bride to be and reply, "Sorry, Mrs. Otter, guess I was
21   daydreaming." So, she should know my name as
22   that's happened hundreds of times.
23 COREY: I'm sure that's made a great impression with her.
24 RYAN: Look! She's looking over here. *(Smiles and waves.)*
25   Hi! Hi! Hi!
26 COREY: Ryan, you're making a fool out of yourself.
27 RYAN: No I'm not. *(Waves.)* Hi, Nicole!
28 COREY: *(Pulls his hand down.)* Stop! Why don't you quit
29   doing that since she's not waving back at you?
30 RYAN: I'm trying to get her attention. *(Waves.)* Hi, Nicole!
31   Hi!
32 COREY: You're getting her attention all right, but I'm not
33   sure it's the kind you're looking for.
34 RYAN: *(Yelling towards her)* Guess what?
35 COREY: Ryan, what are you doing?

1   RYAN: *(Yelling)* You're going to marry me one day!

2   COREY: Why did you do that?

3   RYAN: *(Yells.)* Is that a yes?

4   COREY: I think it was a *no* seeing that she gave you a
5   weird look and turned away.

6   RYAN: *(Yells.)* Wait! We can go on a date first! OK? Do you
7   want to?

8   COREY: I think that's a no.

9   RYAN: Why is she ignoring me? *(Yells.)* I love you, Nicole!

10   COREY: Stop it! Stop it right now!

11   RYAN: But I love her.

12   COREY: And off she goes in the black Mustang. Guess she
13   has a lunch date with that guy.

14   RYAN: Well, this is just great.

15   COREY: So listen, it may hurt for a while, but you'll be OK.

16   RYAN: What's great is that I have class with her after
17   lunch. What am I supposed to do now? Show up to
18   class and pretend I didn't just ask her to marry me?

19   COREY: *(Nods.)* I think so. Or ...

20   RYAN: Or?

21   COREY: Or go into class laughing and say, "I just love a
22   good dare! That was great!"

23   RYAN: Yes! That's what I'll do. That is ... after I wipe the
24   tears off my face. Let me try this. *(Crying)* " I just love
25   a good dare! That was great!" *(Cries loudly.)*

26   COREY: Come on. You'll be fine.

27   RYAN: I hope so.

34. Running through the Halls

CAST: MR. CARSON, HUNTER
SETTING: School hallway

1　*(At rise, MR. CARSON hollers at HUNTER who is caught*
2　*running down the hallway at school.)*
3　**MR. CARSON: Hunter! Come back here right now.**
4　**HUNTER: Yes sir?**
5　**MR. CARSON: Why are you running through the halls? We**
6　**don't do that at Lincoln High.** *(Or say the actual school's*
7　*name.)*
8　**HUNTER: I don't mean to be disrespectful, Mr. Carson, but**
9　**why not? Walk, skip, jog, run ... does it really matter?**
10　**MR. CARSON: It does matter. It's called respect.**
11　**HUNTER: Running is disrespectful?**
12　**MR. CARSON: It's called rules. We don't need a bunch of**
13　**heathens running through the school halls.**
14　**HUNTER: But what if I'm about to be late?**
15　**MR. CARSON: Then you better step it up a notch. But no**
16　**running. Or better yet ... maybe you need to stop**
17　**running your mouth between classes and go straight to**
18　**class when the bell rings.**
19　**HUNTER: I don't do that, Mr. Carson. But what if I just like**
20　**to get my blood flowing between classes?** *(Jogs in place.)*
21　**You know, after sitting in a chair for fifty-five minutes**
22　**or so, I need to move around. Get the heart pumping so**
23　**the brain can become alert so I'll do well in my next**
24　**class.**
25　**MR. CARSON: Then I suggest you walk briskly to class.**
26　**Studies have shown that a brisk walk has health**
27　**benefits similar to running. Without the wear and tear**

1   on your joints ... or being disrespectful!

2 HUNTER: But running feels good.

3 MR. CARSON: *(Mocking him)* But it feels good! So do you

4   think people should just do whatever feels good?

5 HUNTER: No comment.

6 MR. CARSON: Exactly. So, like I said, no running through

7   the halls.

8 HUNTER: But what if I had to go ... really bad ... if you

9   know what I mean.

10 MR. CARSON: Then I'd say don't wait so long next time.

11   Besides, it's not good for your bladder to hold it all

12   day. I know some kids do that. Hold it all day. And all

13   I can ask is why?

14 HUNTER: But what if I saw my girlfriend ahead of me and

15   she's mad at me and I've got to reach her before my

16   next class? And I have a long note to give to her and —

17 MR. CARSON: A note?

18 HUNTER: Yes sir.

19 MR. CARSON: Hogwash!

20 HUNTER: Excuse me?

21 MR. CARSON: You teenagers don't write notes anymore.

22 HUNTER: We don't?

23 MR. CARSON: No! You text. All day long! Behind your

24   backpacks, under your notebooks ... some kids can

25   even text in their pocket without even looking at

26   their phone. At least that's what I've heard.

27 HUNTER: I don't text at school. We're not supposed to.

28 MR. CARSON: Right! Like I believe that one.

29 HUNTER: But we get into trouble for texting during class.

30 MR. CARSON: You also get into trouble for running

31   through the halls.

32 HUNTER: But Mr. Carson, what if I was running because

33   it was an emergency?

34 MR. CARSON: Define emergency.

35 HUNTER: A fire?

1   MR. CARSON: The school is not on fire, Mr. Crawford.

2   HUNTER: But what if I heard that one of my friends was

3   going to take a dare and pull the fire alarm? And I was

4   running through the halls as fast as I could to stop

5   him. Because I know someone would rat him out and

6   he'd be in enormous trouble.

7   MR. CARSON: Are you making this up?

8   HUNTER: No sir.

9   MR. CARSON: And you're not going to rat him out, are

10   you?

11   HUNTER: No sir.

12   MR. CARSON: This is great. We have sectionals in band

13   next period for regional competition next week. I

14   don't have time for my students to be standing

15   outside while the fire department shows up to tell us

16   it was a false alarm. Then the entire class period is

17   wasted.

18   HUNTER: Then if you'd just let me go stop him ...

19   MR. CARSON: Go! Go!

20   HUNTER: I can run?

21   MR. CARSON: Go! Go!

22   HUNTER: I'll stop him, Mr. Carson! *(Runs off.)*

23   MR. CARSON: And I'm going to see who you stop. Then

24   someone's going to be in big trouble. *(Runs off to*

25   *follow him.)*

35. Preapproved

CAST: JACK, AARON
PROPS: Letter from a credit card company
SETTING: Jack's bedroom

1   *(At rise, JACK is reading a letter as ARRON enters.)*
2   **JACK: Oh, yes!**
3   **AARON: Good news?**
4   **JACK: Yes! Yes! Oh, yes!**
5   **AARON: What is it? You won some sweepstakes or**
6   **something?**
7   **JACK: You could say that. I was just preapproved for my first**
8   **credit card.** *(Shows him the letter.)* **See? This is the card**
9   **you've been waiting for. Lower rates. No annual fee.**
10   **And look! I can transfer high rate balances from other**
11   **cards.**
12 **AARON: What other cards? I thought you didn't have a**
13   **credit card.**
14 **JACK: I don't, but it's nice of them to offer me a balance**
15   **transfer. Preapproved. Yes!**
16 **AARON: Dang. And you don't even have a job.**
17 **JACK: How perfect it this?**
18 **AARON: Do you have a credit card limit?**
19 **JACK: Let's see ...** *(Looks at the letter, then excitedly)* **Twenty-**
20   **five hundred dollars!**
21 **AARON: Wow!**
22 **JACK: Christmas has come early! Video games? Yes. That**
23   **sports watch I wanted? Yes. iPad, iPhone ... anything I**
24   **want? Yes.** *(Lifts letter heavenward.)* **Thank you, God!**
25 **AARON: Uh, Jack ... I don't think God sent you that**
26   **preapproved credit card.**
27 **JACK: Well, thank you, if you did. I bet you don't have a**
28   **credit card, do you, Aaron?**

1   AARON: No. Like you, I don't have a job. Maybe when I get
2   my drivers license and I'm making some moolah I
3   can apply for a card. But I heard it's hard to get a
4   credit card without any credit these days.
5   JACK: Well, it wasn't for me. I guess the credit card people
6   saw what a deserving person I was.
7   AARON: I don't know if that's what it was.
8   JACK: Cash or credit? *(As if handing AARON his credit card.)*
9   Charge it to my card, please. Cha-ching, cha-ching,
10   cha-ching! Whatever I want is at my fingertips. I'll
11   take that and that and that ... and *that. (To AARON)* Do
12   you want one?
13   AARON: One what?
14   JACK: I don't know. Anything. An iPad?
15   ARRON: Sure I want one.
16   JACK: *(As if handing over his card)* I'll take two of those,
17   please. Just charge it to my card.
18   AARON: Thanks, Jack.
19   JACK: That's what friends are for.
20   AARON: Uh, question. How are you going to pay your
21   credit card bill when it comes in?
22   JACK: What?
23   AARON: The bill. You know, you have to pay for all that
24   stuff you just pretended to charge. Not to mention the
25   interest those companies tack on.
26   JACK: Interest? *(Looks at the letter.)* Look. Zero percent
27   interest for six months. I like that.
28   AARON: But that's not zero payments. You will be getting
29   a bill for all those purchases you make.
30   JACK: Oh. I hadn't thought about that.
31   AARON: So you're sitting there with your new video
32   games, your new iPad, listening to the new music you
33   downloaded and your mom walks into your room
34   and drops a bill on your desk. You open it up and talk
35   about a holy moly moment. You've gone over your

1   credit limit by a few hundred dollars so those nice
2   credit card people have added on over-limit fees.
3   Which cancels out your zero percent interest for six
4   months and now you have twenty-seven-point-nine
5   percent interest tacked on and your first minimum
6   payment of three hundred dollars is due on the first
7   of the month. So, how are you going to handle that?
8   JACK: A three-hundred-dollar payment?
9   AARON: Or more. Those penalty fees and interest can kill
10 you. And don't even think about paying your bill late
11 because those late fees are horrendous! Then you
12 might be looking at a huge monthly payment ... for
13 years!
14 JACK: For years?
15 AARON: Then you keep shopping and charging and they
16 keep adding on those fees and interest and the late
17 charges and before long, you'll be in so much debt
18 before your sophomore year that you'll have to drop
19 out of school and get a job.
20 JACK: But I don't want to do that.
21 AARON: Well, as my parents say, don't buy what you can't
22 afford. Cash is king.
23 JACK: Wow. I never thought about the payments.
24 AARON: It'll ruin your life, Jack. Then you'll be calling
25 Dave Ramsey.
26 JACK: Who's that?
27 AARON: Financial counselor. Anyway, you'll be calling
28 Dave Ramsey and he'll tell you to cut up that credit
29 card immediately, get three jobs if that's what it takes
30 to get out of debt, eat beans and rice if that's all you
31 can afford, and no more eating out or shopping.
32 Every dollar has a name!
33 JACK: Huh?
34 AARON: You will probably need to cancel the cable and sit
35 in the dark. Because now, you're going to live like no

1   one else, so later you can live like no one else. Which
2   means, get out of debt! Then you'll be calling his
3   radio show screaming, "I'm debt free!" But it took
4   you three years of eating beans and rice and sitting in
5   the dark with no cable. *(Pats his back.)* But if that's
6   what you want to do, I support you my friend.

7 JACK: No way am I doing that! *(Tears up the letter.)* I don't
8   want payments. I don't want to live a life of worry
9   wondering how I'm going to pay my credit card bill. I
10   don't want to quit school and get a job. And I sure
11   don't want to eat beans and rice for three years.
12   *(Continues to rip up the letter.)* No, thank you.

13 AARON: Good decision.

14 JACK: And I think I'll call that Dave Ramsey guy today.

15 AARON: What for?

16 JACK: To tell him this. *(Screams.)* ***I'm debt free!***

36. Fashion Police

CAST: VICTOR, SETH
SETTING: Coffee shop

1 (At rise, SETH is dressed in sloppy, wrinkled clothes.
2 VICTOR enters.)
3 **VICTOR: Whoa! What is this?**
4 **SETH: What? What are you talking about?**
5 **VICTOR: You.**
6 **SETH: Me?**
7 **VICTOR: Your clothes.**
8 **SETH: What's wrong with my clothes?**
9 **VICTOR: You're actually brave enough to wear that in**
10   **public?**
11 **SETH: What? Is my shirt on backwards?** (Looks.) **No. Shoes**
12   **match. Socks match. What's the problem?**
13 **VICTOR: Sloppy. Wrinkled. And in a word ... blasé.**
14 **SETH: Blasé?**
15 **VICTOR: Yes, you are. Sloppy, wrinkled, and blasé.**
16 **SETH: I call it comfortable.**
17 **VICTOR: You look like you just crawled out of bed.**
18 **SETH: I did. I mean, I didn't sleep in my clothes, but I just**
19   **grabbed the first thing I could find.**
20 **VICTOR: Seth, how can you expect to impress someone**
21   **looking like that?**
22 **SETH:** (Shrugs.) **I'm not trying to impress anyone.**
23 **VICTOR: Obviously.**
24 **SETH: Who would I want to impress?**
25 **VICTOR: Your mentors.**
26 **SETH: Who?**
27 **VICTOR: How about your teachers?**
28 **SETH: Nah. They don't care what I wear to school unless it's**
29   **indecent. And I'm not showing any skin.**

1   VICTOR: How about impressing your boss at work?

2   SETH: I don't need to do that. I work in the back of the

3   store unloading trucks that come in. I can't wear nice

4   clothes or I'll mess them up.

5   VICTOR: Your parents?

6   SETH: Seriously?

7   VICTOR: Girls?

8   SETH: Girls? Well, maybe ...

9   VICTOR: You know, girls prefer a well-dressed man. Take

10   me, for example.

11 SETH: You look pretty ordinary if you ask me.

12 VICTOR: Wrinkle free. Color coordinated. I'd say I look

13   sharp.

14 SETH: Sharp. Who dresses sharp these days? And I haven't

15   seen any girls hanging all over you lately.

16 VICTOR: Actually ... I have three dates tonight.

17 SETH: Three? Are you serious?

18 VICTOR: One at six, one at seven-thirty, and one at nine.

19 SETH: You're giving them an hour and a half each?

20 VICTOR: An hour. I need time in between to drop off and

21   pick up.

22 SETH: But why so many dates? Why not pick out one and

23   skip all the running around town picking up three

24   different dates?

25 VICTOR: They asked me out. I have a hard time saying no.

26 SETH: And it's all because of the way you dress?

27 VICTOR: Seth, sloppy and wrinkled does not scream

28   charm and debonair. It screams unintelligent

29   scumbag who's lazy and boring.

30 SETH: Don't forget blasé.

31 VICTOR: And blasé. Seth, if you want the women to like

32   you, then you must impress them. Save the sloppy,

33   comfortable look for weekends at home.

34 SETH: So you're saying I should spiff it up a bit?

35 VICTOR: I'd say a lot. That is ... if you want my advice.

1 SETH: Hmmmm ... I might just give it a shot. Not for my
2   teachers or parents, but for the girls ... Yeah, I would
3   like to impress a few beauties I've actually had my
4   eyes on. And the truth is, they never seem to notice
5   me.
6 VICTOR: Then pick it up a notch. Dress to kill.
7 SETH: I thought girls only did that.
8 VICTOR: Who has three dates tonight?
9 SETH: Yeah. I guess I do need to dress to kill.
10 VICTOR: *(Looks at his watch.)* Well, I've got to go. First date
11   in thirty minutes. Think about what I said. *(Exits.)*
12 SETH: Dress to kill? I can do that. From blasé to ... *(Does a*
13   *little move.)* You're looking at the next hottie out
14   there. Guess I better go to the mall and do some
15   shopping.

37. Academic Award

CAST: JOHN, SEAN
PROPS: Tissues
SETTING: School hallway

1   *(At rise, SEAN enters and finds JOHN's face in his hands,*
2   *crying.)*
3   **SEAN: John, are you crying?**
4   **JOHN:** *(As he cries.)* **No!**
5   **SEAN: Yes, you are.**
6   **JOHN: No, it's allergies.**
7   **SEAN: Lisa break up with you?**
8   **JOHN: No.**
9   **SEAN: Parents getting a divorce?**
10   **JOHN: No.**
11   **SEAN: Pet died?**
12   **JOHN: No.**
13   **SEAN: Failed a class? No pass, no play?**
14   **JOHN: No.**
15   **SEAN: Then why are you crying?**
16   **JOHN:** *(Blows nose.)* **My mom ...**
17   **SEAN: She's dying?**
18   **JOHN: No!**
19   **SEAN: You had a fight with her?**
20   **JOHN: No.**
21   **SEAN: She hurt your feelings?**
22   **JOHN: No. I miss her!**
23   **SEAN:** *(Gives him a strange look.)* **You miss your mom?**
24   **JOHN: Yes!**
25   **SEAN:** *(Looks around.)* **Dude, pull it together! What if**
26   **someone sees you?**
27   **JOHN: I'm trying!**
28   **SEAN: Well, if you miss your mom so much, why don't you**

1   go home and see her? Problem solved. But this ...
2   crying in the hallway for your mommy ... dude, you're
3   too old for that.
4 JOHN: I know!
5 SEAN: Then go home and see her.
6 JOHN: I can't!
7 SEAN: Why not?
8 JOHN: She's not home.
9 SEAN: Oh ... She left? Abandoned her family? I've heard of
10   moms doing that. Wake up one morning and decide
11   they don't like their life anymore. Pack their bags
12   and they're like, "I'm outta here!" Party! No more
13   cooking, cleaning, laundry, disrespectful brats. No
14   more slaving away for an unappreciative family. "See
15   ya later, alligators! 'Cause Mommy is leaving and
16   she's never coming back. Time to live it up! Par-ty!
17   Par-ty!" *(Does a little dance move.)*
18 JOHN: That's not what happened. My mom is out of town.
19   She's taking care of my sick Aunt Betty.
20 SEAN: Oh. She didn't leave to *par-ty?*
21 JOHN: No. But she's been gone for a month now and I ...
22 SEAN: You miss your mom.
23 JOHN: Yes! *(Blows nose.)*
24 SEAN: Well, she'll be back.
25 JOHN: *(Crying)* I know. But Thursday I'm getting an award
26   in academics and I wanted her to be there.
27 SEAN: Can your dad go?
28 JOHN: No, he has to work. So I'll be ... *(Trying not to fall*
29   *apart.)* All alone!
30 SEAN: OK, OK, it'll be all right.
31 JOHN: But I want my mom there. She's never missed any
32   of my programs at school. And she's always the mom
33   in the front row that claps the loudest.
34 SEAN: I'll tell you what ...
35 JOHN: What?

1   SEAN: I'll be there! And I'll clap really loud ... just like your
2   mom. Like this ... *(Claps loudly.)* "Way to go, John! I'm
3   so proud of you, son!" *(As if talking to someone next to*
4   *him.)* "That's my baby boy up there! I'm so proud of
5   him!"
6   JOHN: Don't do that.
7   SEAN: Yeah, I guess I better not, but I can act like a mom.
8   *(Claps.)* Moms do always clap the loudest.
9   JOHN: Well, it won't be the same.
10 SEAN: John, your mom would be there if she could.
11 JOHN: I know.
12 SEAN: So you've got to gut it up. Take it like a man.
13 JOHN: I'm trying. *(Wipes away a tear.)*
14 SEAN: Be the man your mom would want you to be. Stand
15   tall. Stand proud and represent your family as you
16   receive your academic award.
17 JOHN: OK. I'll do that.
18 SEAN: And when you accept your certificate you can look
19   to the audience and say, "This is for you, Mom!" Give
20   it a try.
21 JOHN: OK. *(As if holding up a certificate.)* "This is for you,
22   Mom."
23 SEAN: That was great.
24 JOHN: And I love you, Mom. And I miss you. Oh, Mom, I
25   miss you so much! *(Cries.)*
26 SEAN: Oh, no! You can't do that. We're going to have to
27   work on this. Let's not thank Mom after all. How
28   about you say, "To me, for all my hard work." Because
29   after all, you are the one who did it.
30 JOHN: Yeah, that might be better.
31 SEAN: So ... here's your certificate. *(As if handing it to him.)*
32 JOHN: Thank you.
33 SEAN: And what will you say?
34 JOHN: I want to thank myself for working hard.
35 SEAN: Good. A little self-appreciation is good.

1   JOHN: *(As if speaking to the audience)* **And to you, Mom.**

2   **For having me. For giving birth to me. For loving me.**

3   **Changing my diapers, training me up the way I**

4   **should go ... I love you, Mom. I love you so much!**

5   SEAN: *(Pulling him off the pretend stage)* **And we'll just exit**

6   **right here.**

7   JOHN: *(Hollering)* **I love you, Mom! I miss you!**

8   SEAN: **I sure am glad we have a couple of days to work on**

9   **this.**

10 JOHN: **I miss you, Mom. Come home. Please, come home!**

11   *(Cries.)*

12 SEAN: *(Pulls him Off-Stage.)* **I've got my work cut out for**

13   **me.** *(As they exit)* **Leave your mom out of this. Just**

14   **thank yourself for all your hard work.** *(JOHN cries*

15   *loudly.)*

38. Love Song

CAST: MICHAEL, ROBERT
PROPS: Pad of paper, pen
SETTING: Robert's bedroom

1 *(At rise, MICHAEL enters ROBERT's bedroom.)*
2 **MICHAEL:** Hey Robert, what are you working on?
3 **ROBERT:** I'm writing a song.
4 **MICHAEL:** Seriously?
5 **ROBERT:** I only have a few lines so far. Do you want to hear
6   it?
7 **MICHAEL:** Sure.
8 **ROBERT:** "You are my dream come true, you make me
9   smile. You don't know I'm alive, but I'm in love with
10   you." What do you think?
11 **MICHAEL:** Hmmmm ... Maybe it'd sound better if it you sang
12   it.
13 **ROBERT:** You don't like it?
14 **MICHAEL:** It just sounds like a poem instead of a song.
15 **ROBERT:** Well, I'm going to finish writing it. Then I'll put
16   music to it.
17 **MICHAEL:** You write music, too?
18 **ROBERT:** No, but my cousin Sheila does and she said she'd
19   help me out. And then when I have it all put together,
20   I'm going to sing it to Lilly on Valentine's Day.
21 **MICHAEL:** Where? At school?
22 **ROBERT:** I guess. Unless I go to her house and knock on her
23   door. But what if her dad answers?
24 **MICHAEL:** But how are you going to sing it to her at school
25   with everyone watching and listening?
26 **ROBERT:** Well, Lilly and I have chemistry together so I
27   thought I'd ask her to help me on a project. Mr. Jimenez
28   pretty much lets us do our own thing, so then we can

1   stand in the corner and I'll sing her my song.

2 MICHAEL: In chemistry?

3 ROBERT: Yes. That's the only class Lilly and I have

4   together. Unless I sing it to her in the lunchroom and

5   it'd be really crowded in there. Talk about not having

6   any privacy.

7 MICHAEL: Or you could sing it to her over the school

8   intercom.

9 ROBERT: Do you think they'd let me? Seeing that it was

10   Valentine's Day?

11 MICHAEL: No. But I have a better idea.

12 ROBERT: What's that?

13 MICHAEL: Say you did and don't.

14 ROBERT: Huh?

15 MICHAEL: Robert, don't make a fool out of yourself.

16 ROBERT: Michael, I'm trying to be romantic here.

17 MICHAEL: You just said in your song that Lilly didn't

18   know you were alive.

19 ROBERT: And hopefully my song will show her that I am.

20 MICHAEL: Or not. She may wish you were dead after this.

21 ROBERT: Stop being so negative. Michael, you don't have

22   a romantic bone in your body.

23 MICHAEL: That is true. I'm not the lovey-dovey feeling

24   type of guy.

25 ROBERT: So I have this tune in my head. Do you want to

26   hear it?

27 MICHAEL: Robert, how about you make your song into a

28   poem instead? Then you can just drop it into her

29   locker. And to make it even more romantic, sign it

30   "From your secret admirer."

31 ROBERT: Secret admirer? Why would I want to do that? I

32   want Lilly to know I'm alive and that I'm in love with

33   her. And I want to tell her in the most romantic way

34   possible.

35 MICHAEL: Poems are romantic.

1   **ROBERT:** *(Begins to sing badly, screeching.)* **"You are my**
2   **dream come true, you make me smile. You don't**
3   **know I'm alive, but I'm in love with you."**
4   **MICHAEL: No, Robert! Don't do it. I know. You can buy her**
5   **one of those Valentine-grams and have it sent to her**
6   **class. Girls love those! And sign your name if you**
7   **want to.**
8   **ROBERT: That is so ordinary. Everyone does that. I want**
9   **our first Valentine's Day to be special. Lilly and I**
10   **standing in the chemistry room and I remove my**
11   **goggles, look at her like this ...** *(Demonstrates)* **and I**
12   **tell her I have a surprise for her. She smiles, her eyes**
13   **gleaming as she looks at me with anticipation. And**
14   **then I sing her a song. "You are my dream come true,**
15   **you make me smile. You don't know I'm alive, but I'm**
16   **in love with you."**
17   **MICHAEL: Robert, please. Don't do it. You're going to**
18   **make a fool out of yourself.**
19   **ROBERT: I don't think so, Michael. Girls like romance.**
20   **But most guys aren't brave enough to pull off**
21   **something romantic like this. So, I'm writing Lilly a**
22   **love song. And ... I need to get finished. So ... do you**
23   **mind? I need to concentrate here.**
24   **MICHAEL: Don't say I didn't warn you.**
25   **ROBERT: Warning noted.** *(MICHAEL exits.)* **Love shall**
26   **prevail!** *(Sings.)* **"You are my dream come true, you**
27   **make me smile. You don't know I'm alive, but I'm in**
28   **love with you." Let's see. What could be next?** *(Stares*
29   *at his notepad and thinks for a moment.)* **Oh! I know.**
30   *(Sings.)* **"From the moment you asked to borrow some**
31   **paper from me, and I lent it to you ... You smiled at me**
32   **... Oh yes, that's when I knew, yes, that's when I knew**
33   **I was in love with you!"**

39. Grandma Car

CAST: AUSTIN, JERRY
SETTING: Outside of school

1 AUSTIN: Hey Jerry, why do you look so depressed?
2 JERRY: Oh, I found out that my dad is buying me a car.
3 AUSTIN: You're depressed about that? I'd be like jumping
4   up and down for joy. I have a bike.
5 JERRY: The car my dad is buying me cost six hundred and
6   fifty dollars.
7 AUSTIN: Oh. Have you seen it?
8 JERRY: Two words. Grandma car.
9 AUSTIN: Ah, man! But it has low mileage, right?
10 JERRY: Sure, but it's a hundred years old. Four doors. Tan.
11   And huge. I mean huge! Nothing sporty about it. It has
12   grandma written all over it.
13 AUSTIN: Dang.
14 JERRY: Honestly, I'd rather walk.
15 AUSTIN: Why don't you tell your dad it's just not what you
16   had in mind.
17 JERRY: I did! I said, "Dad, no. Get me a used Mustang or
18   sport utility or anything else ... but that!"
19 AUSTIN: What did he say?
20 JERRY: He said, "Son, I'm buying the car and I'm paying for
21   the insurance so you get what you get."
22 AUSTIN: You get what you get?
23 JERRY: That's what he said. I get what I get.
24 AUSTIN: When do you get it?
25 JERRY: Today.
26 AUSTIN: Well, just wear a hat and some sunglasses and duck
27   if you see any of your friends from school. Other than
28   that, enjoy your freedom. At least you won't have to
29   depend on your parents to give you a ride to school

1   anymore like I do.

2   JERRY: I know, but I was so excited about having my first

3   car and I never imagined it'd be a grandma car.

4   AUSTIN: Maybe you can make it look more sporty.

5   JERRY: How?

6   AUSTIN: Put some cool stickers on the bumper and back

7   windshield. You know like a skull and crossbones.

8   JERRY: My mom wouldn't let me put that on my car. She'd

9   say it was satanic or something like that.

10   AUSTIN: OK, forget the skulls, but you can find something

11   else. Like a Harley Davidson sticker. Those are really

12   cool.

13   JERRY: Sure, sure. Slap a Harley Davidson sticker on my

14   grandma car. That'll make me look cool.

15   AUSTIN: And maybe you could hang some big chains from

16   the rearview window. And I know! You could tint the

17   windows.

18   JERRY: I like that idea. Then no one could see me. But

19   that's expensive.

20   AUSTIN: My uncle does that at his shop. And with you

21   being my friend, he'd work out something with you.

22   He did that for one of his friend's son and he let him

23   pay it off by working in the shop.

24   JERRY: That'd be awesome! Tint the windows really dark,

25   add some cool stickers, some chains, then maybe

26   later I could buy some cool rims.

27   AUSTIN: Does it have a CD player?

28   JERRY: Are you kidding? It has a cassette player.

29   AUSTIN: Wow. That is an old car.

30   JERRY: Tell me about it.

31   AUSTIN: Do you even have any cassettes?

32   JERRY: *(Sarcastically)* No, but I'm sure I could hit up a few

33   garage sales and find some Neil Diamond or Barry

34   Manilow cassettes.

35   AUSTIN: OK, next you'll need a good stereo system. One

1   step at a time.

2 JERRY: Dad said he's counting on me to wreck my first

3   car. Or at least back into something and dent it up

4   good.

5 AUSTIN: Kyle hit a dumpster last week.

6 JERRY: I heard about that.

7 AUSTIN: And Natalie tore off her side mirror at Sonic

8   when she backed up.

9 JERRY: I wouldn't do that.

10 AUSTIN: And Sid hit a tree last week.

11 JERRY: How'd he hit a tree?

12 AUSTIN: I don't know. He just said he didn't see it. It came

13   at him from out of nowhere.

14 JERRY: I heard that Matt backed over his sister's bike.

15 AUSTIN: And what about Shane totaling his car on

16   Fifteenth Street? Pulled right out in front of

17   someone.

18 JERRY: Well, I'm not going to wreck my grandma car.

19   Although ... Oh, never mind.

20 AUSTIN: Then you'd be back to riding a bike. Like me.

21 JERRY: Yeah. So you want a ride to school tomorrow?

22 AUSTIN: Sure. But will it hurt your feelings if I wear a hat

23   and sunglasses?

24 JERRY: No. I'll be doing the same thing.

25 AUSTIN: And after school we can go to my uncle's shop

26   and see about getting your windows tinted.

27 JERRY: That'd be great! And I'm going to tell him I want

28   them as dark as possible.

29 AUSTIN: I would, too.

30 JERRY: Because I sure don't want anyone seeing me

31   driving a grandma car to school.

32 AUSTIN: Man, parents sure do know how to kill a kid's

33   reputation.

34 JERRY: Tell me about it.

40. Forgery

CAST: DEREK, ALEX
PROPS: Report card, pen, paper
SETTING: Outside of school

1   DEREK: Alex, can you write in cursive?
2   ALEX: No. Who does that? I text. I email. And I print on
3   paper when I'm forced to.
4   DEREK: Could you try?
5   ALEX: You want me to write in cursive?
6   DEREK: Yeah. And make it look pretty with curly lines.
7   ALEX: Curly lines?
8   DEREK: You know — like girls do.
9   ALEX: Why would I want to write in cursive like a girl?
10 DEREK: Scratch girl. My mom.
11 ALEX: Oh! You want me to forge your mom's signature?
12 DEREK: You got it.
13 ALEX: Bad grade?
14 DEREK: Try bad report card.
15 ALEX: Your mom has to sign it? They e-mailed a copy of it to
16   my parents.
17 DEREK: Dad's overseas and Mom doesn't have e-mail. She's
18   way behind on the times. She still writes letters if you
19   can believe that.
20 ALEX: So you need your mom's signature? I can try. (Grabs a
21   pen.) Where do you want me to sign?
22 DEREK: Wait! You should practice first. (Hands him a piece
23   of paper.) Here. Practice on this.
24 ALEX: OK. Cursive is kind of like printing, isn't it? You just
25   don't pick up your pen between the letters. Let's see ...
26   Let me try this ... (He writes.) How's that?
27 DEREK: That's terrible. It doesn't look anything like my
28   mom's signature. Plus you wrote your name.

1 ALEX: That's because I don't know your mom's name. Let
2   me try again. What's her name?
3 DEREK: Helen Sawyer.
4 ALEX: OK. Let me try. Pretty, curly lines ... I can do this.
5   *(Writes.)* Helen Sawyer. How's that?
6 DEREK: That's not bad.
7 ALEX: I knew I could do it. So give me your report card
8   and I'll sign away.
9 DEREK: Wait. Can you practice a few more times and try
10   to add a few more curly lines to her signature?
11 ALEX: Sure. I can do that. *(Writes.)* Curly little lines. How's
12   that?
13 DEREK: That's perfect!
14 ALEX: For someone who never learned cursive, you have
15   to admit I did a pretty good job.
16 DEREK: Alex, I'm impressed. No one would ever know
17   that wasn't my mom's signature.
18 ALEX: Except for your mom.
19 DEREK: True.
20 ALEX: So are you ready for me to do this?
21 DEREK: I think so. Here you go. *(Hands him the report*
22   *card.)* Remember the pretty curly lines.
23 ALEX: *(Writes on the report card.)* Looks good to me. What
24   do you think?
25 DEREK: *Alex!*
26 ALEX: What? What's wrong?
27 DEREK: You wrote *your* name! Alex Malone!
28 ALEX: *(Looks at the report card.)* Oops. I sure did. Now why
29   did I do that?
30 DEREK: Why did you do that, Alex?
31 ALEX: Well, probably because I'm used to writing my own
32   name.
33 DEREK: But you'd been practicing writing my mom's
34   name!
35 ALEX: I know. That's just weird, isn't it? But you have to

1   admit; it looks good, doesn't it? Do you like the way I
2   put the little curly lines in "Malone"? *(Writing in the*
3   *air)* Alex Malone. I think it's pretty. You know, I might
4   start writing in cursive all the time.
5 DEREK: Pretty? Are you serious?
6 ALEX: Yeah! I think it's pretty.
7 DEREK: It's your name on my report card, you idiot.
8 ALEX: Oops. Can we white it out?
9 DEREK: Alex, you know the minute I white it out, the
10   school will become suspicious and call my mom.
11 ALEX: That's true. What are we going to do, Derek?
12 DEREK: I don't know, Alex.
13 ALEX: I know. Go to the office and tell them you lost your
14   report card. See if they will give you another one.
15 DEREK: They won't. It comes from the downtown office.
16   They'd just send in a new request and mail it to my
17   mom instead. And I'm sure they'd call my mom about
18   the delay, too.
19 ALEX: Then what are we going to do?
20 DEREK: I don't know. Take a chance that they think Alex
21   Malone is my mom?
22 ALEX: You could try.
23 DEREK: You bozo! That'd never work.
24 ALEX: I know.
25 DEREK: What?
26 ALEX: *(Dramatically)* The truth will set you free.
27 DEREK: No, the truth will get me grounded.
28 ALEX: *(Shrugs, casually.)* Either way, it sounds like you're
29   in trouble.
30 DEREK: True.
31 ALEX: Then take my advice.
32 DEREK: Tell the truth? Tell my mom I had you forge her
33   name, but it ended up being your name and then I
34   decided I should just fess up and face the
35   consequences?

1   ALEX: Yes. And add, "I love you, Mom!" And throw in
2   some tears. *(Demonstrates.)* "I love you, Mom! *(Cries.)*
3   Please tell me that you still love me too, because if
4   you don't, I can't go on. *(Cries louder.)* I'm a dummy,
5   Mom! A complete dummy!"
6 DEREK: Hey!
7 ALEX: "But Mom, I promise to start studying harder from
8   now on. I promise, Mom. Cross my heart. Oh, Mom ...
9   please forgive me!"
10 DEREK: Oh, brother! *(Starts off.)*
11 ALEX: *(Falls to his knees.)* "Mom, I'm sorry!"
12 DEREK: *(Looks back at him.)* Never! *(Exits.)*
13 ALEX: *(Still on his knees.)* "But Mom, I'm sorry. Please
14   forgive me. I'm such a dummy! *(Bends over and hits
15   his head on the floor.)* A genuine, bona fide dummy."
16   *(Continues to pound his head on the floor. After a
17   moment, he stands up.)* Well, that's what I'd do if I
18   were you.

41. Running Lines

CAST: CONNOR, LOGAN
PROPS: Two play scripts
SETTING: Logan's bedroom

1   CONNOR: Why do I have to do this?
2   LOGAN: Connor, I need help learning my lines for the play.
3   CONNOR: Just memorize them.
4   LOGAN: I'm trying. But if you could read the other person's
5   lines it'd help me.
6   CONNOR: But I'm not good at drama. But put me in a
7   football helmet ... yeah! That's what I do. But drama?
8   Please.
9   LOGAN: Connor, you don't have to do any acting. I just need
10   you to read the lines for me. OK?
11 CONNOR: OK, fine. *(Takes the script.)* So who am I?
12 LOGAN: *(Points to the script.)* This is you.
13 CONNOR: Lilly? I have to be a girl?
14 LOGAN: You're just reading the lines, Connor.
15 CONNOR: But I don't really like reading a girl's part.
16 LOGAN: Just do it to help me out. OK?
17 CONNOR: Do you want me to sound like a girl? *(Girl's voice)*
18   Like this? Do you want me to talk like a girl?
19 LOGAN: No. Just read the lines for me.
20 CONNOR: Logan, you're going to owe me one for this, you
21   know it?
22 LOGAN: OK, I owe you. *(Points to the script.)* Let's start right
23   here.
24 CONNOR: *(Reads from script.)* "Stop pressuring me, Phillip.
25   I can't think when you do that to me." *(Looks away from
26   the script.)* Yeah, that sounds like a girl all right.
27 LOGAN: Connor, don't add any of your comments. I have to
28   get this memorized.

1   CONNOR: Sorry. *(Reads from script.)* **"Stop pressuring me,**
2   **Phillip. I can't think when you do that to me."**
3   LOGAN: **"Lilly, you have to choose."**
4   CONNOR: **"Phillip, why can't you understand how hard**
5   **this is for me?"**
6   LOGAN: **"What about how hard it is for me?"**
7   CONNOR: **"It's hard for both of us!"**
8   LOGAN: **"Then make a decision, Lilly."**
9   CONNOR: *(Crosses arms.)* **"I can't decide."**
10 LOGAN: **"You can't."**
11 CONNOR: **"No."**
12 LOGAN: **"Then I'll decide for you."**
13 CONNOR: **"What do you mean by that?"**
14 LOGAN: **"Just what I said. I'll make it easy on you, Lilly."**
15 CONNOR: *(Looks away from script.)* **Logan, can I skip the**
16   **next line?**
17 LOGAN: **Keep going, Connor. Keep going!**
18 CONNOR: *(Deep breath)* **"But I love you, Philip."**
19 LOGAN: **"Obviously not enough, Lilly."**
20 CONNOR: **"No, no, I do! I love you!"** *(Looks away from*
21   *script.)* **OK, this is creeping me out.**
22 LOGAN: **"Then prove it!"**
23 CONNOR: **Prove that it's creeping me out?**
24 LOGAN: **No! Read the next line.**
25 CONNOR: **"I will prove it!"**
26 LOGAN: **"How?"**
27 CONNOR: *(Dryly)* **"I pick you, Phillip. You're the one I**
28   **want to be with. Not Matt or anyone else."** *(To*
29   *LOGAN)* **Can we stop now?**
30 LOGAN: *(Ignoring him)* **"You pick me over Matt?"**
31 CONNOR: **"Yes."**
32 LOGAN: **"Promise?"**
33 CONNOR: **"Yes, I promise"**
34 LOGAN: *(Adoringly)* **"Oh, Lilly ... "**
35 CONNOR: *(Looking at the script, he takes a big step*

1   *backwards.)* **Whoa! We're not embracing!**
2   **LOGAN: "Tell me you love me, Lilly."**
3   **CONNOR:** *(Shakes head.)* **I can't.**
4   **LOGAN: Read the script, Connor.**
5   **CONNOR:** *(Takes a deep breath, then dryly.)* **"I love you,**
6   **Phillip. You and no other."**
7   **LOGAN: "Oh, Lilly!"**
8   **CONNOR:** *(Steps back again.)* **And I'm not doing this either.**
9   **This ... this kissing scene! No siree! You have to**
10   **actually do this onstage? In front of everyone?**
11   **LOGAN: With Chelsea. I'm not complaining. And it's just a**
12   **little peck.**
13   **CONNOR: You get to kiss Chelsea?**
14   **LOGAN: Yes. She's playing the part of Lilly.**
15   **CONNOR: Ah, man. You lucky dog. Where can I sign up for**
16   **drama?**
17   **LOGAN: Connor, I wouldn't do that if I were you.**
18   **CONNOR: Why not?**
19   **LOGAN: Honestly?**
20   **CONNOR: What? You think I stink at acting?**
21   **LOGAN: Yes.**
22   **CONNOR: Hey, I can act. Watch this. "I love you, Lilly! I**
23   **love you and no other." Did you see that? Did you see**
24   **my sincerity? "I love you, Lilly! I love you and no**
25   **other."**
26   **LOGAN: Connor, now you're creeping me out.**
27   **CONNOR: But I was acting. Don't you think I'm good at it?**
28   **LOGAN: Uh ... no.** *(Exits.)*
29   **CONNOR: "But I love you! I love you and no other!" I**
30   **thought that was pretty good.**

Man and Woman

42. Lucky Penny

CAST: ELIZABETH, JOSEPH
PROPS: Two pennies
SETTING: Sidewalk

1   *(At rise, ELIZABETH picks up a penny from the ground.)*
2 **ELIZABETH: Hey, look what I found.**
3 **JOSEPH: Whoop dee doo.**
4 **ELIZABETH: Find a penny, pick it up, the rest of the day**
5   **you'll have good luck.**
6 **JOSEPH: I think they need to change that saying.**
7 **ELIZABETH: Change it how?**
8 **JOSEPH: Find a dollar, pick it up ...**
9 **ELIZABETH: A dollar?**
10 **JOSEPH: A penny's not worth anything these days. You**
11   **might as well throw it away.**
12 **ELIZABETH: No!**
13 **JOSEPH: You can't buy anything with it.**
14 **ELIZABETH: With several of them I can.**
15 **JOSEPH: Yeah, like ninety-nine more of them and maybe**
16   **you could buy a pack of gum.**
17 **ELIZABETH: I don't care. I still feel lucky when I find a**
18   **penny.**
19 **JOSEPH: I'd feel lucky if I found a dollar.**
20 **ELIZABETH: Do you know what I can do with this penny**
21   **that you can't do with a dollar bill?**
22 **JOSEPH: What?**
23 **ELIZABETH: Toss it in the fountain and make a wish.**
24 **JOSEPH: I could toss a dollar in the fountain.**
25 **ELIZABETH: No one does that.**
26 **JOSEPH: Why not? Maybe my wish would actually come true**
27   **if I put in more money than a stinking penny.**
28 **ELIZABETH: Sure, then you'd have people scampering into**

1   the fountain to grab your dollar bill so your wish

2   wouldn't come true.

3   JOSEPH: Oh, who believes in wishes from a fountain

4   anyway?

5   ELIZABETH: You know what, Joseph? You're no fun. And

6   I'm keeping my lucky penny and I think something

7   wonderful will happen to me today.

8   JOSEPH: That reminds me. Did you see the cast list that

9   Mr. Morton posted at the end of the day?

10   ELIZABETH: He did! He posted it already? I thought he

11   wasn't posting it until in the morning.

12   JOSEPH: Me too, but he went ahead and stuck it outside

13   the drama room, then left. You didn't see it?

14   ELIZABETH: No! Tell me. Tell me quick.

15   JOSEPH: *(Casually)* You got the lead.

16   ELIZABETH: The lead? I did? I get to play Juliet?

17   JOSEPH: You do.

18   ELIZABETH: I knew it! My lucky penny worked.

19   JOSEPH: And guess who got the part of Romeo?

20   ELIZABETH: Oh, tell me Carter. Please, please, please tell

21   me Carter. *(Holds her penny up in the air.)*

22   JOSEPH: *(Casually)* Carter.

23   ELIZABETH: Yes! Oh, yes, yes! *(Kisses her penny.)* I'm

24   saving this penny forever. My lucky penny. And you

25   know what? The day is not over yet.

26   JOSEPH: Elizabeth, your penny has nothing to do with you

27   getting the lead role in the play. It's called talent.

28   Either you have it or you don't.

29   ELIZABETH: And I have it. *(Kisses penny.)* Oh, thank you,

30   lucky penny.

31   JOSEPH: *(Shakes head.)* So, do you have a date to the

32   homecoming dance?

33   ELIZABETH: Not yet. I really hate to go alone, don't you?

34   JOSEPH: Well, not to ruin anything for you, but when me

35   and Romeo, that is me and Carter, were checking out

1   the cast list outside the drama room, Carter said he
2   was going to call his Juliet tonight and invite her to
3   the dance.
4 ELIZABETH: What? Are you serious? You swear that's
5   what he said?
6 JOSEPH: That's what I heard him say.
7 ELIZABETH: *(Jumping up and down)* Carter's asking me to
8   the dance! I can't believe it. Oh my gosh!
9 JOSEPH: Yeah, unless there's another girl at school
10   named Juliet, I think he'll be calling you tonight.
11 ELIZABETH: Oh my gosh! Carter's asking me to the
12   dance. And I got the lead of Juliet and he'll be my
13   Romeo. *(Holds up her penny.)* Thank you, lucky
14   penny!
15 JOSEPH: It's not the penny, Elizabeth.
16 ELIZABETH: Yes it is.
17 JOSEPH: It's just a coincidence.
18 ELIZABETH: I don't think so.
19 JOSEPH: So what time are you and your dad coming by
20   the store on Saturday?
21 ELIZABETH: What makes you think my dad and I are
22   coming up to your work on Saturday? We don't need
23   to buy any parts for a car.
24 JOSEPH: I didn't mean the parts department, but to look
25   at cars.
26 ELIZABETH: For what?
27 JOSEPH: For your birthday.
28 ELIZABETH: My dad's going to buy me a car for my
29   birthday?
30 JOSEPH: He didn't tell you?
31 ELIZABETH: No!
32 JOSEPH: Oh, man. I didn't know it was a surprise. Your
33   dad asked me to tell him which car salesman I would
34   recommend him talking to on Saturday.
35 ELIZABETH: I'm getting a car for my birthday?

1   JOSEPH: Hey, hey, you didn't hear it from me. OK?

2   ELIZABETH: Could this day get any better?

3   JOSEPH: If you won like a million dollars.

4   ELIZABETH: Do you suppose Publishers Clearinghouse is

5   at my door this very minute?

6   JOSEPH: Not unless you entered the sweepstakes.

7   ELIZABETH: I did! I actually did.

8   JOSEPH: Couldn't happen.

9   ELIZABETH: I bet you wished you had my lucky penny.

10   JOSEPH: Nah.

11   ELIZABETH: Well, I'm sure glad I found it. *(Kisses the*

12   *penny.)* Thank you, lucky penny!

13   JOSEPH: *(Looks down.)* Hey, what's that?

14   ELIZABETH: What?

15   JOSEPH: That. *(Picks up a penny.)*

16   ELIZABETH: You found one, too!

17   JOSEPH: *(Smiles, holding out his penny.)* Find a penny, pick

18   it up, the rest of the day, you'll have good luck.

19   ELIZABETH: It worked for me.

20   JOSEPH: Yes. Maybe it will for me, too. I hope so. *(They*

21   *exit.)*

43. The Power of Words

CAST: MELANIE, ROBBY
PROPS: Folded notebook paper
SETTING: Outside of school

1   *(At rise, MELANIE is twirling around with her arms*
2   *outstretched. ROBBY is watching her.)*
3   **MELANIE: It's snowing!**
4   **ROBBY: No it's not.**
5   **MELANIE:** *(Still twirling)* **Yes it is.**
6   **ROBBY: No. It's not.**
7   **MELANIE: Well, it's about to. I love the snow. I'm going to**
8   **run through it. And I'm going to stick my tongue out**
9   **and taste the snowflakes. And I'm going to make a**
10   **snowball and throw it at you.**
11 **ROBBY: Did you just get off the phone with the**
12   **weatherman? Because I don't see a single snowflake.**
13 **MELANIE: No, but I read somewhere that you can speak**
14   **things into existence. Our words are very powerful, you**
15   **know.**
16 **ROBBY: Speak things into existence, huh? Like I have**
17   **passed this geometry test?** *(Holds up a folded paper.)*
18 **MELANIE: Exactly. Say it again and mean it.**
19 **ROBBY:** *(Holds up paper.)* **I have passed this geometry test.**
20   **Gosh, I hope I really have.**
21 **MELANIE: You haven't looked at your grade yet?**
22 **ROBBY: No. I was afraid. Folded it up and decided to deal**
23   **with it later. I'm barely passing geometry and a failing**
24   **test grade will send me over the edge. To a place my**
25   **parents will make sure I never want to visit again.**
26 **MELANIE: Do you want me to look at the test for you?**
27 **ROBBY: No, because I'm afraid I'll be able to tell if I passed**
28   **or failed by the look on your face.**

163

1   MELANIE: Hey, look. A snowflake!

2   ROBBY: Wow! It sure is. So maybe that positive talk does
3   work after all. Kind of like you are what you eat,
4   except you are what you speak.

5   MELANIE: It's true, Robby. So if you go around saying I'm
6   dumb, I'm stupid, and everyone hates me, then your
7   actions will follow and people won't like you and
8   you'll do poorly in school. But if you speak positive
9   words, that's how you will feel about yourself and
10   your actions will follow.

11 ROBBY: You wanted it to snow and look, more snowflakes
12   are falling.

13 MELANIE: Like I said, I heard that our words are very
14   powerful.

15 ROBBY: I wonder if this could really work for me?

16 MELANIE: Of course it can.

17 ROBBY: *(Holding up his test paper)* I passed the geometry
18   test. I passed. I passed. I passed.

19 MELANIE: Did you study?

20 ROBBY: No.

21 MELANIE: But did you feel good about the test?

22 ROBBY: No.

23 MELANIE: Well, are you going to look at it?

24 ROBBY: No.

25 MELANIE: Why not?

26 ROBBY: I'm scared.

27 MELANIE: Well, next time maybe you should add some
28   action to your words.

29 ROBBY: What do you mean?

30 MELANIE: When you are studying, tell yourself you're
31   going to remember what you've learned and you're
32   going to pass the test.

33 ROBBY: I'd rather skip the studying and just wish it into
34   existence.

35 MELANIE: Robby, it doesn't work that way.

1 ROBBY: It did when you wished for snow. And now it's
2   snowing.
3 MELANIE: But that was different.
4 ROBBY: No it wasn't. I'm a believer now too. Yes! I like this
5   speaking things into existence. *(Yells.)* It's snowing!
6   And look. Yes, it is! *(Yells.)* I passed my geometry test!
7   And ... *(Unfolds his paper and looks at it.)*
8 MELANIE: And? *(Pause)* Did you pass?
9 ROBBY: No.
10 MELANIE: You should've studied.
11 ROBBY: Yeah. So much for speaking things into existence.
12 MELANIE: Well, sometimes it takes action, too.
13 ROBBY: I guess.
14 MELANIE: Don't give up, Robby. Give it another try.
15 ROBBY: OK. *(Looks at MELANIE.)* You're going to kiss me.
16 MELANIE: What?
17 ROBBY: Hey, I'm speaking it into existence. You're going
18   to kiss me.
19 MELANIE: *(Looks at him.)* In your dreams. *(Exits.)*
20 ROBBY: Hey! In my dreams? *(Thinks about this.)* Hmmmm
21   .... Maybe she means she's going to kiss me in my
22   dreams tonight. That might not be so bad. *(Exits.)*

44. ID Required

CAST: DONNA, BRANDON
PROPS: Cell phone, walkie talkie
SETTING: Outside a nightclub

1   *(At rise, BRANDON is about to enter a nightclub when*
2   *DONNA stops him.)*
3   **DONNA: I need to see your ID.**
4   **BRANDON:** *(Deep voice)* **Don't worry about it. I'm twenty-**
5   **one.**
6   **DONNA: ID please.**
7   **BRANDON: What? You don't think I look twenty-one?**
8   **DONNA: No.**
9   **BRANDON: You've got to be kidding me.**
10 **DONNA:** *(Holds out her hand.)* **ID please.**
11 **BRANDON: Look, I'm twenty-one, OK?**
12 **DONNA: You look fourteen.**
13 **BRANDON: Well, I'll take that as a compliment. I'm sure**
14   **when I get old, that will work well in my favor.**
15 **DONNA: ID please.**
16 **BRANDON: Seriously? Can't you see that I'm twenty-one?**
17 **DONNA: Seriously, you look fourteen.**
18 **BRANDON: This is crazy. I've just graduated from college.**
19   **I'm living on my own. Paying my own bills, but you**
20   **won't let me go into this nightclub?**
21 **DONNA: No. Not without an ID.**
22 **BRANDON: Look, I don't drink. I'm against drinking. I just**
23   **want to go inside and check the place out. See what it's**
24   **all about.**
25 **DONNA: After you show me your ID, you can do that.**
26 **BRANDON: You are just one tough security person, aren't**
27   **you?**
28 **DONNA: It's my job.**

1 BRANDON: Well, let's make a deal. Let me go inside for a
2   few minutes to see what it's like in there, maybe snap
3   a few pictures for my friends to see ... and maybe
4   check myself in on Facebook ... Ten minutes then I'm
5   out of there.
6 DONNA: Stay in there all night if you want to. They don't
7   close until four a.m. But you're not getting in without
8   an ID. So let me see your ID. But I seriously doubt you
9   are twenty-one.
10 BRANDON: Twenty-one going on twenty-two!
11 DONNA: Right. ID please.
12 BRANDON: *(Reaches to his back pocket.)* Ah, man.
13 DONNA: Let me guess. You forgot your ID.
14 BRANDON: Would you believe that?
15 DONNA: Yes. And I also believe that you're fourteen years
16   old.
17 BRANDON: Fourteen? Are you serious?
18 DONNA: You look fourteen to me.
19 BRANDON: That is the craziest thing I've ever heard.
20   Fourteen? That'd make me a baby.
21 DONNA: So, what's your real age, then?
22 BRANDON: I told you. I'm twenty-one.
23 DONNA: Liar.
24 BRANDON: I am! I'm twenty-one.
25 DONNA: Whatever. You're not going in the club without
26   an ID.
27 BRANDON: Oh, please! Just long enough to snap a few
28   pictures and say I was there?
29 DONNA: Why would you want to do that?
30 BRANDON: So I can look cool to all my friends.
31 DONNA: At twenty-one you're still worried about looking
32   cool to your friends?
33 BRANDON: Well, yeah ...
34 DONNA: Let me tell you something. *(Grabs him by the shirt*
35   *collar.)* You don't need to go into a place like that to be

1   cool. Do you hear me?

2   BRANDON: Dang! You sound like my mom.

3   DONNA: Listen here, there are wild people in there acting

4   out of control. Women scantily dressed ... hitting on

5   every man who walks through that door.

6   BRANDON: Oh! I want to see that.

7   DONNA: And don't you care about your reputation?

8   BRANDON: I don't know. I was just trying to find

9   something to brag about. Like, look what I did this

10   weekend. Opposed to cleaning my room and

11   sweeping out the garage.

12 DONNA: You should be ashamed of yourself. Trying to get

13   into a place like this ... *(Shakes her head.)*

14 BRANDON: Yeah, well you're starting to make me feel

15   ashamed. Thanks a lot.

16 DONNA: *(Grabs him by his shirt collar.)* How old are you?

17 BRANDON: Sixteen.

18 DONNA: I knew it!

19 BRANDON: No, you said you thought I was fourteen.

20 DONNA: I knew you weren't twenty-one. And I knew you

21   weren't old enough to get into a nightclub.

22 BRANDON: OK, OK, you caught me.

23 DONNA: And that's my job here. To keep people like you

24   out of places like this. Now get out of here and don't

25   let me see your face around here again.

26 BRANDON: Wait! Could I ask you to do me a little favor

27   before I leave?

28 DONNA: What?

29 BRANDON: Well, if I can't go inside I can at least check

30   myself in on Facebook and post a picture. Everyone

31   will be like, "Wow, you went *there* this weekend?"

32   And I'll casually say, "Yeah, I sure did." That won't be

33   a lie. I am here, aren't I? So would you take a picture

34   of me standing in front of the club? Here, you can use

35   my phone. *(Offers his phone to her.)*

1 DONNA: No. Forget it.
2 BRANDON: Fine, then I'll just have to check myself in on
3   Facebook. I mean, I am here ... *(Looking at his phone)*
4 DONNA: *(Grabs him by his collar.)* You are trying my
5   patience. Do you want me to call the police?
6 BRANDON: The police? No! No! Please don't do that.
7 DONNA: I will if that's what it takes. I'll have them escort
8   you off these premises ... in handcuffs.
9 BRANDON: Handcuffs? No, no, I'm leaving! But are you
10   sure you won't take just one picture of me first?
11   Standing right here in front of the club?
12 DONNA: *(Into a walkie talkie)* I need some backup here on
13   Fifth and Main. I have a juvenile who needs to be
14   taken into custody.
15 BRANDON: Yikes. I'm leaving! *(Runs off.)* See you when
16   I'm twenty-one.
17 DONNA: And don't come back! *(Shakes her head.)* Kids.

45. Mind Reader

CAST: NICOLE, KEVIN
SETTING: Outside of school

1 NICOLE: Kevin, I want to ask you something.
2 KEVIN: OK.
3 NICOLE: Are you ready?
4 KEVIN: I guess.
5 NICOLE: Wait. Before I ask, I want you to know that if you
6   don't say yes, I will absolutely die.
7 KEVIN: Wow. That's a lot of pressure, Nicole.
8 NICOLE: So please, please, please say yes.
9 KEVIN: But what if I can't?
10 NICOLE: Kevin, you have to.
11 KEVIN: But what if I don't want to?
12 NICOLE: Kevin, sometimes we do things we don't want to
13   do.
14 KEVIN: Not me. If I don't want to, I don't do it.
15 NICOLE: Homework?
16 KEVIN: I only do homework because I don't want to deal
17   with summer school.
18 NICOLE: Well, anyway ... please, please, please say yes.
19 KEVIN: Nicole, why don't you ask me so I'll know if I can say
20   yes?
21 NICOLE: Oh please, don't say no. Because if you say no I will
22   completely fall apart.
23 KEVIN: Nicole, you're starting to scare me.
24 NICOLE: I'm the one who's scared.
25 KEVIN: Of what?
26 NICOLE: Of your answer.
27 KEVIN: Well, why don't you ask me so you can know the
28   answer?
29 NICOLE: Wait! I'm going to practice first.

1   KEVIN: Practice asking me your question?
2   NICOLE: Yes, but not out loud. *(Pause)*
3   KEVIN: What are you doing? Asking me in your head?
4   NICOLE: Yes, that's what I'm doing.
5   KEVIN: And did I answer you in your head?
6   NICOLE: No, but let's try this again. *(Pause as she stares at*
7   *him)* So, what's your answer?
8   KEVIN: I don't know. I didn't hear the question.
9   NICOLE: OK, listen. This time when I'm mentally asking
10   you the question, see how you feel. *(Pause as she*
11   *stares at him)* So, what do you think?
12   KEVIN: I think I'm confused.
13   NICOLE: But did you feel like saying yes or no?
14   KEVIN: Neither, because I didn't hear the question.
15   NICOLE: OK, let's try this one more time.
16   KEVIN: Why?
17   NICOLE: Just once more. But this time, let's hold hands.
18   *(She reaches out and they hold hands.)* Now, Kevin,
19   look deeply into my eyes.
20   KEVIN: *(Losing his patience)* I'm looking.
21   NICOLE: No, look deeper.
22   KEVIN: I'm looking, Nicole!
23   NICOLE: Now in my mind, I'm going to ask you my
24   question. See if you can feel how you should answer.
25   *(Pause as she stares at him.)* Well?
26   KEVIN: Yes.
27   NICOLE: *(Excited)* You will?
28   KEVIN: Yes.
29   NICOLE: *(Hugs him.)* Thank you! Thank you! Thank you!
30   KEVIN: You're welcome. I think.
31   NICOLE: Oh, I can't wait! We're going to have so much
32   fun. Aren't you excited?
33   KEVIN: Thrilled.
34   NICOLE: Me too! And to think you just read my mind.
35   KEVIN: Who would've thought ...

1   NICOLE: Oh, Kevin. It's fate. It's magical. It's unbelievable!

2   KEVIN: Yes, unbelievable, all right.

3   NICOLE: So don't forget. Friday night at seven p.m.

4   KEVIN: Seven p.m.

5   NICOLE: Meet me here.

6   KEVIN: OK.

7   NICOLE: And bring a coat because it's going to be cold.

8   *(Smiles.)* But we can snuggle.

9   KEVIN: Wait a minute. Just to clear things up ... you know,

10   to make sure I understand ... What did I just say yes

11   to?

12 NICOLE: Going with me on the fall hayride. And you did

13   say yes. You and me and ... and ... I'm so excited.

14 KEVIN: Yeah, that sounds fun.

15 NICOLE: Thanks for saying yes, Kevin.

16 KEVIN: Well, thank you for asking me and letting me read

17   your mind.

18 NICOLE: Hey, do you want to try it again?

19 KEVIN: Sure.

20 NICOLE: OK. Give me your hands. *(They hold hands.)* Now,

21   look deeply into my eyes. *(Pause)* What am I thinking?

22 KEVIN: You're thinking that you hope I kiss you on the

23   hayride.

24 NICOLE: *(Excited)* How did you know?

25 KEVIN: *(Shrugs.)* I guess I can read minds after all.

26 NICOLE: Well, it's OK with me.

27 KEVIN: What? Reading your mind or kissing you on the

28   hayride?

29 NICOLE: *(Smiles at him.)* Both.

46. Cheapskate

CAST: LUIS, ELLA
PROPS: Plastic sack with receipt, candle, candy, and dental
floss
SETTING: Ella's front porch

1   *(At rise, LUIS is holding a plastic sack.)*
2   **LUIS:** *(Holds the sack out to ELLA.)* **Sorry I didn't wrap your**
3   **birthday present.** *(Hands her the sack.)*
4   **ELLA:** *(Not happy)* **Really? Are you kidding me?**
5   **LUIS:** *(Shrugs.)* **I didn't have any wrapping paper.**
6   **ELLA:** *This* **is the best you could do?**
7   **LUIS: Sorry.**
8   **ELLA: It looks to me like you ran to the store, grabbed a**
9   **quick gift, and then just left it in the plastic sack.** *(Looks*
10   *inside and pulls out a receipt.)* **Oh, and here's your**
11   **receipt, Luis.**
12 **LUIS:** *(Grabs the receipt.)* **Give me that! How'd this get in**
13   **there?**
14 **ELLA:** *(Looking inside the sack)* **A candle, package of candy ...**
15   *(Pulls out dental floss)* **and dental floss? Really? Dental**
16   **floss?**
17 **LUIS:** *(Grabs the dental floss.)* **Oops. That was mine. Not**
18   **yours. Gotta keep those gums healthy, you know.**
19 **ELLA: Wow.**
20 **LUIS: Do you like the candle?**
21 **ELLA: I'm amazed.**
22 **LUIS: You are?**
23 **ELLA: Yes. I'm amazed that you didn't put any effort into my**
24   **birthday gift. Ran into the store ... I'm assuming the**
25   **dollar store ... bought a cheap candle, a package of off-**
26   **brand candy, and dental floss.**
27 **LUIS: The dental floss wasn't yours, Ella. But you can have it**

1   if you want it. *(Offers it to her.)*

2   ELLA: I don't want your stupid dental floss. But pearls or

3   diamonds ... ?

4   LUIS: You wanted pearls?

5   ELLA: Or diamonds.

6   LUIS: But Ella, my budget is a bit scarce for that.

7   ELLA: Well, you could've saved for it.

8   LUIS: But we've only been dating a few weeks. How was I

9   supposed to save that much money so fast?

10 ELLA: I don't know, Luis. *(Holds up the sack.)* But this?

11   Really? And it's not even wrapped.

12 LUIS: It's the thought that counts, right?

13 ELLA: Luis, there was no thought to this. You walked into

14   the dollar store for some dental floss and thought,

15   "Oh yeah, I need to buy my girlfriend a birthday gift."

16   So you grabbed a couple of quick things and you were

17   done. Gee, thanks.

18 LUIS: No, that's not the way it was, Ella. I went into the

19   store ... and it wasn't the dollar store ... to buy you a

20   birthday gift and then I thought, "Oh yeah, I need to

21   buy some dental floss." *(Offers it to her again.)* But you

22   can have it I if you want it. Really. I don't mind.

23 ELLA: I don't want your stupid dental floss, Luis.

24 LUIS: But it's cinnamon.

25 ELLA: I don't care.

26 LUIS: Ella, you should care about your gums.

27 ELLA: I do care about my gums, Luis. But I don't want

28   dental floss as a birthday gift!

29 LUIS: I was just offering ...

30 ELLA: No! Talk about *not* being romantic.

31 LUIS: Ella, I don't really get that romantic thing.

32 ELLA: Obviously.

33 LUIS: But if it'd help, I'll take you out for a birthday

34   dinner. Would you like that?

35 ELLA: Well, maybe. Where would you take me?

1   LUIS: To the Taco Stand on Fifth Street.

2   ELLA: The Taco Stand?!

3   LUIS: Yeah! On Tuesdays you get two tacos for a dollar and
4   I have enough for us to get two each.

5   ELLA: The Taco Stand? Are you serious? You want to
6   spend one dollar on my birthday dinner?

7   LUIS: Don't you like tacos?

8   ELLA: Of course I like tacos, but I was thinking something
9   more romantic like a fine Italian restaurant. Maybe I
10   could order the roasted eggplant mozzarella ravioli
11   or the clam and crab pasta ...

12   LUIS: Whoa! I can't afford that. I've only got a couple of
13   bucks. And that kind of restaurant is expensive.

14   ELLA: So you're telling me you will take me to the Taco
15   Stand for my birthday?

16   LUIS: Yes I am.

17   ELLA: After handing me a plastic sack with a cheap
18   candle and off-brand candy?

19   LUIS: Sorry I didn't wrap it.

20   ELLA: Not to mention you left the receipt in the bag. With
21   your dental floss!

22   LUIS: *(Offers her the floss.)* It's still yours if you want it.

23   ELLA: And there are no pearls or diamonds?

24   LUIS: *(Laughs.)* You think I could afford that?

25   ELLA: *(Looking at the sack)* And this is it?

26   LUIS: *(Smiles.)* That's it.

27   ELLA: Luis ...

28   LUIS: Yes, Ella?

29   ELLA: You're a lousy gift buyer.

30   LUIS: Yeah ...

31   ELLA: And you're cheap.

32   LUIS: Yeah, but it's because I'm broke.

33   ELLA: And I'll let you take me to the Taco Stand on Fifth
34   Street, but only because I'm hungry and I'm broke,
35   too.

1   **LUIS: Great! Let's go.** *(As they start off, he sings)* **"Happy**

2   **Birthday to you ... "**

47. The Petition

CAST: JENNIFER, MR. CLARK
PROPS: Ruler, petition, code of conduct
SETTING: Principal's office

1 (*At rise, MR. CLARK, the principal, is seated at his desk.*
2 *JENNIFER stands in front of him holding a petition.*)
3 **JENNIFER: Mr. Clark, I would like to speak to you on behalf**
4 **of myself and the other students.**
5 **MR. CLARK: Well, make it snappy. I have fourteen students**
6 **in the hallway waiting to see me.** (*Slaps a ruler across his*
7 *desk.*) **I miss those days when I could say, "Bend over**
8 **and take it like a man ... or woman." Then ...** (*Slams*
9 *ruler on desk three times.*) **There! You may leave now.**
10 **They come in, they go out, but rarely did I see that same**
11 **kid again. Not after this.** (*Hits the ruler on his desk three*
12 *times.*) **Now, do you think they're afraid of a little**
13 **afterschool detention for playing with their cell phones**
14 **underneath their backpacks? No siree. Hmmmm ... I**
15 **wonder what would happen if I ignored the school**
16 **policy and actually whacked the next student who**
17 **entered my office. Like this!** (*Hits the ruler on his desk*
18 *three times.*) **"Now get out of here and don't let me see**
19 **you again!"**
20 **JENNIFER: Me?**
21 **MR. CLARK: Not you.** (*Points to the door.*) **Them! Now, what**
22 **are you in here for? Something about a petition?**
23 **JENNIFER: Yes sir. I'm here as a spokesman ... well,**
24 **spokeswoman ... on behalf of the students at Bowie**
25 **High.**
26 **MR. CLARK: Oh, goody. Can't wait to hear this.**
27 **JENNIFER:** (*Waves the petition in the air.*) **I have a petition.**
28 **MR. CLARK:** (*Waves a notebook in the air.*) **And I have the**

1   school's code of conduct. Wanna compare?

2 JENNIFER: Mr. Clark, I have four hundred and twenty-two

3   signatures.

4 MR. CLARK: Well, that was a waste of time.

5 JENNIFER: Mr. Clark, you can't ignore the signatures.

6 MR. CLARK: Wanna bet?

7 JENNIFER: These signatures represent the demands of

8   the students here at Bowie High.

9 MR. CLARK: *(Slams ruler on desk.)* For what? Longer lunch

10   periods? More time between classes? Change the

11   dress code policy? I don't think so. But what I'd like to

12   change in this code of conduct is to allow the

13   principal to give you licks. Just like in the good ole

14   days. Because back in the good ole days, we just

15   busted their behinds. Took care of the problem right

16   then and right there.

17 JENNIFER: Back to my petition ...

18 MR. CLARK: Do I have to listen to this?

19 JENNIFER: Yes. I insist.

20 MR. CLARK: Go ahead, then. Let me hear this. But make it

21   fast. As I said before, I have fourteen students outside

22   waiting to speak to me about behavioral problems,

23   and since I can't do this ... *(Hits ruler on desk)* I must

24   find a way to make them fear me. *(Hits ruler on desk.)*

25   Do you fear me?!

26 JENNIFER: Uh ... sure.

27 MR. CLARK: Sure?

28 JENNIFER: Yes sir.

29 MR. CLARK: That's better.

30 JENNIFER: Back to my petition ... Mr. Clark, I respectfully

31   present this petition to you on behalf of four hundred

32   and twenty-two students in hopes that you will

33   reconsider the dress code policy.

34 MR. CLARK: I knew it!

35 JENNIFER: How did you know?

1 MR. CLARK: Same thing every year. You kids want to wear
2   what you want to wear.
3 JENNIFER: Which we all feel we should be able to do.
4 MR. CLARK: Hats?
5 JENNIFER: Yes sir.
6 MR. CLARK: Shorts?
7 JENNIFER: Yes sir.
8 MR. CLARK: Flip-flops?
9 JENNIFER: Yes sir.
10 MR. CLARK: Bathing suits?
11 JENNIFER: Well, maybe not bathing suits.
12 MR. CLARK: Pajamas?
13 JENNIFER: Well, maybe pajama pants. They are
14   comfortable.
15 MR. CLARK: Hand the petition to me, Miss Brown. *(She*
16   *hands him the petition.)* **You have wasted a lot of time**
17   **collecting these signatures between classes and**
18   **during lunch periods.**
19 JENNIFER: I disagree. And I stand firm with our desire to
20   have an open school dress policy.
21 MR. CLARK: I'm sure you do. But guess what?
22 JENNIFER: What?
23 MR. CLARK: It's not going to happen. *(Picks up the*
24   *notebook.)* **Dress code policy will remain the same.**
25 JENNIFER: But that's not fair.
26 MR. CLARK: Life's not fair, Miss Brown. You should be
27   spending your time and energy studying ... not
28   collecting signatures for things that aren't going to
29   change.
30 JENNIFER: Then maybe I'll take my petition to the school
31   board.
32 MR. CLARK: Be my guest. And you know what? I might
33   just go with you to that meeting.
34 JENNIFER: Why?
35 MR. CLARK: To see about reinstating the rules for

1   punishment. **Back in my day, we did this!** *(Hits ruler*
2   *on desk.)* **And that's what I'd like to do again. Over and**
3   **over again!** *(Continues to hit the ruler on the desk.)*
4   **JENNIFER:** *(As she exits.)* **See you at the school board**
5   **meeting, Mr. Clark.**
6   **MR. CLARK: I'll be there. Bend over and take this, you**
7   **disrespectful student!** *(Hits ruler on desk.)*

48. Consequences

CAST: MARIA, DIEGO
PROPS: Book
SETTING: Living room

1   *(At rise, MARIA sits in the living room reading a book.*
2   *Her brother, DIEGO enters from the front door and*
3   *tiptoes past her. He does not see MARIA.)*
4   **MARIA:** *(Watching DIEGO tiptoe past her)* **Where have you**
5   **been?**
6   **DIEGO:** *(Jumps.)* **Oh! You scared me.**
7   **MARIA: Where have you been?**
8   **DIEGO: Shhhh!**
9   **MARIA: Mom said you were already in bed.**
10   **DIEGO: Don't worry about it.**
11   **MARIA: That's funny. I even peeked into your room. I was**
12   **looking for a book. Your lights were out and I saw you**
13   **in your bed.**
14   **DIEGO: Well, I ... uh ... woke up and went for a walk.**
15   **MARIA: No you didn't, because I've been here by the front**
16   **door all night. You faked Mom out by stuffing pillows**
17   **in your bed and turning out the lights, didn't you?**
18   **DIEGO: Don't worry about it.**
19   **MARIA:** *(Loudly)* **You snuck out!**
20   **DIEGO: Shhhh!**
21   **MARIA:** *(Looks at her watch.)* **It's after midnight. Where have**
22   **you been?**
23   **DIEGO: Are you going to rat me out?**
24   **MARIA: I don't know. Maybe. I haven't decided. Wasn't it**
25   **just last week that you ratted me out about having**
26   **three of my friends in my car when I'm only allowed**
27   **one person at a time?**
28   **DIEGO: Maria, I was thinking of your safety.**

1   MARIA: Yeah, right. Well, I'll be thinking of your safety too
2   when I tell Mom you snuck out of the house and were
3   roaming around the dangerous streets until after
4   midnight.
5   DIEGO: No! You can't.
6   MARIA: Sure I can.
7   DIEGO: Look, I'll owe you one, OK?
8   MARIA: One?
9   DIEGO: Two! I'll owe you two.
10 MARIA: Nah. I'd rather see you face some consequences
11   big brother. Just like I did. I can't drive for thirty days
12   now thanks to you tattling on me, so ... I wonder what
13   Mom will do to you?
14 DIEGO: Kill me!
15 MARIA: Then I could have your room. Yes. It's bigger than
16   mine. And I've always wanted it. Can I have your
17   computer and TV, too? I'm sure I can. Mom won't
18   care.
19 DIEGO: Maria, come on. Work with me here.
20 MARIA: Or maybe Mom will put one of those devices on
21   your leg. You know an ankle monitor like they do for
22   people who are on probation. That way she could
23   keep track of your every move. To school, then home.
24   To school, then home. Because that's all you'd be
25   doing. To school, then home.
26 DIEGO: Mom wouldn't put an ankle monitor on me.
27 MARIA: Wanna bet? Chad's mom did it to him.
28   Remember? Mom said if Chad were her son, she
29   would too. "Gotta get control of these kids one way or
30   the other." That's what she said.
31 DIEGO: So what do you want, Maria? Name it.
32 MARIA: Now we're talking. I like this. Hmmmm ... Watch
33   you limp around the house with an ankle monitor or
34   name my price ... Hmmmm ... Decisions, decisions ...
35 DIEGO: OK, I shouldn't have snuck out. But the guys

1   wanted me to go hang out and I knew Mom wouldn't

2   let me on a school night, so ...

3 MARIA: So you snuck out and did what you wanted?

4 DIEGO: Hey, you have no room to talk. You snuck around

5   with your car crammed full of friends when Mom

6   specifically said only one person at a time was

7   allowed in your car for the first six months.

8 MARIA: And, Diego, I would've gotten away with it had it

9   not been for *you* ratting me out.

10 DIEGO: Which means I owe you big time, Maria. I've

11   learned my lesson about keeping my mouth shut and

12   now I'm going to pay up.

13 MARIA: Oh, yes you are.

14 DIEGO: So, what do you want?

15 MARIA: Well, for starters ... a foot massage.

16 DIEGO: What?

17 MARIA: My feet hurt. It's been a long day.

18 DIEGO: Are you serious?

19 MARIA: Yes.

20 DIEGO: No.

21 MARIA: Shall I go wake Mom up?

22 DIEGO: No!

23 MARIA: *(Smiles at him.)* Foot massage, please.

24 DIEGO: *(Begins to massage her foot.)* I hate you.

25 MARIA: I hate you, too. Oh, that feels good. A little harder,

26   please.

27 DIEGO: Your feet stink.

28 MARIA: No, they don't. You're just saying that.

29 DIEGO: No ... *(Waves hand in front of face.)*

30 MARIA: OK! OK! That's enough.

31 DIEGO: Thank you.

32 MARIA: Next you can bring me a snack.

33 DIEGO: Bring you a snack?

34 MARIA: Yes. I'd like a peanut butter sandwich, please.

35   With sliced bananas. And make sure you slice the

1   bananas really thin. That's the way I like it. With lots

2   of crunchy peanut butter.

3 DIEGO: Are you serious?

4 MARIA: Yes. Then after that, I'd like you to paint my nails.

5 DIEGO: What?

6 MARIA: It's hard for me to paint them myself. And I have

7   this new pink color I want to try out. You can do that

8   for me after I finish my midnight snack. And hand

9   me the remote control on your way to the kitchen.

10 DIEGO: Maria, this isn't fair.

11 MARIA: I think it's plenty fair. And tomorrow you can do

12   my math homework for me. And my daily chores.

13   Which tomorrow is Thursday so that means you'll be

14   picking up the dog poop in the backyard. Oh, and

15   cleaning the guest bathroom. And then —

16 DIEGO: *(Suddenly yells out.)* Mom!

17 MARIA: What are you doing?

18 DIEGO: I'm turning myself in. I'd rather deal with Mom's

19   consequences than yours. *(As he exits)* Mom, I have a

20   confession! Mom! Mom! I love you, Mom!

49. She Loves Me, She Loves Me Not

CAST: CALEB, AUDREY
PROPS: Rose, coin
SETTING: Outside of school

1   *(At rise, CALEB is pulling the petals off a rose.)*

2   **CALEB: She loves me, she loves me not, she loves me, she**

3   **loves me not, she loves me, she loves me not ...** *(Picking*

4   *off the last petal.)* **She loves me!** *(Kisses the petal.)* **Oh,**

5   **Audrey!**

6   **AUDREY:** *(Enters.)* **Hey, Caleb.**

7   **CALEB: Audrey! You ... you ... !**

8   **AUDREY:** *(Gives him a strange look.)* **What? I have something**

9   **on my face? My hair is sticking up? What? What?**

10   **CALEB:** *(Holds out the petal.)* **You love me!**

11   **AUDREY: OK, what do you want, Caleb? You need to borrow**

12   **some money? Need some help with one of your**

13   **assignments? Advice for a girlfriend issue?**

14   **CALEB: Uh ... the latter. Girlfriend issues.**

15   **AUDREY: OK, spill it.**

16   **CALEB: You do love me, don't you?**

17   **AUDREY: Obviously, if I'm volunteering to listen to your**

18   **girlfriend problems. So tell me, what's going on with**

19   **you and ... and what's her name?**

20   **CALEB: Let's just leave her nameless for now. OK?**

21   **AUDREY: OK. So, what's going on with you and your**

22   **nameless girlfriend?**

23   **CALEB: Well, I love her ...** *(Holds out the petal.)* **And she loves**

24   **me.**

25   **AUDREY: And the two of you had a fight?**

26   **CALEB: No, no, not that.**

1   AUDREY: Then what?

2   CALEB: Well, we love each other ...

3   AUDREY: Caleb, I got that part.

4   CALEB: And I've been in love with her since the fourth
5   grade.

6   AUDREY: OK. And ... ?

7   CALEB: Here's the problem, Audrey. She doesn't know
8   that she loves me. Yet, that is. But she does. *(Holds out*
9   *the petal.)* You ... I mean, she ... loves me!

10 AUDREY: But I thought you said you two loved each other.

11 CALEB: We do, but it's complicated.

12 AUDREY: I'm confused.

13 CALEB: Audrey, do you believe in signs?

14 AUDREY: What kind of signs?

15 CALEB: Like flipping a coin. Heads, she loves me, tails she
16   doesn't.

17 AUDREY: No, that's just wishful thinking. And you could
18   flip a coin until you got the right answer.

19 CALEB: But what about a rose?

20 AUDREY: You found your sign in a rose?

21 CALEB: *(Shows her the petals on the ground.)* She loves me,
22   she loves me not, she loves me, she loves me not, she
23   loves me, she loves me not ... *(Holds out his petal.)* She
24   loves me!

25 AUDREY: I see ... So, she's not your girlfriend, but you love
26   her and now you think she loves you, too.

27 CALEB: That's correct. *(Holds out his petal.)* She loves me!

28 AUDREY: I see. And you're basing your theory on that
29   petal?

30 CALEB: Yes! That is correct.

31 AUDREY: And you've never told her how you feel?

32 CALEB: Correct.

33 AUDREY: Then you should.

34 CALEB: I should?

35 AUDREY: Yes. That way you can see if she feels the same

1   way about you.
2 CALEB: When should I tell her?
3 AUDREY: The sooner the better is my advice.
4 CALEB: But how? How do I tell her I love her?
5 AUDREY: *(Takes his hand.)* Take her hand, like this ...
6 CALEB: Yes ...
7 AUDREY: Look deeply into her eyes ...
8 CALEB: *(Looking deeply into her eyes.)* Yes ...
9 AUDREY: And say ...
10 CALEB: And say ...
11 AUDREY: I don't mean to scare you ...
12 CALEB: I don't mean to scare you ...
13 AUDREY: But I must be honest ...
14 CALEB: But I must be honest ...
15 AUDREY: You've captured my heart ...
16 CALEB: You've captured my heart ...
17 AUDREY: And the truth is ...
18 CALEB: And the truth is ...
19 AUDREY: I love you.
20 CALEB: I love you, too!
21 AUDREY: Not me. Her!
22 CALEB: Oh, Audrey, I knew you loved me, too.
23 AUDREY: Not me!
24 CALEB: Yes, you! *(Holds up his petal.)* She loves me, she
25   loves me not, she loves me, she loves me not, she
26   loves me! You love me, Audrey.
27 AUDREY: Me?
28 CALEB: Yes, you. Me and you!
29 AUDREY: Wait a minute? I'm the nameless girlfriend? Or
30   wannabe girlfriend, that is?
31 CALEB: Not anymore. Now you have a name. Audrey!
32 AUDREY: Whoa! Wait a minute.
33 CALEB: *(Holds up the petal.)* Right here. Here's my sign.
34   You love me!
35 AUDREY: I do?

1   **CALEB: You do.**

2   **AUDREY: But I didn't know ...**

3   **CALEB: Now you do.** *(Takes her hand and looks deeply into*

4   *her eyes.)* **Audrey, I don't mean to scare you, but I**

5   **must be honest. You've captured my heart. And the**

6   **truth is, I love you.**

7   **AUDREY: Oh, Caleb ... I really like you, but I just ... .I don't**

8   **know ... I mean ... I don't know what to say ...**

9   **CALEB:** *(Hands her the petal.)* **For you!**

10   **AUDREY: Thank you. But ... I don't know what to say ...**

11   *(Suddenly)* **Look!**

12   **CALEB: What?**

13   **AUDREY:** *(Picks up the rose stem.)* **There's a tiny petal left**

14   **right here.**

15   **CALEB: What? But ... no!**

16   **AUDREY: Guess we don't love each other after all.**

17   **CALEB: But ...**

18   **AUDREY: But I like you.** *(Kisses his cheek.)* **And we will**

19   **always be friends. Hey, I've gotta run. Talk to you**

20   **later.** *(Exits.)*

21   **CALEB:** *(Holding the stem)* **But ...** *(Takes a coin out of his*

22   *pocket and tosses it.)* **Heads she loves me, tails she**

23   **doesn't.** *(Looks at the ground, then picks up the coin.)*

24   **OK, two out of three. Heads she loves me, tails she**

25   **doesn't.** *(Looks at the ground. Smiles.)* **She loves me!**

26   *(Runs off.)* **Audrey, come back! You do love me!**

50. Overpowering

CAST: PATRICK, BAILEY
SETTING: School hallway

1 *(At rise, BAILEY walks past PATRICK.)*
2 PATRICK: Woo wee! I could smell you coming.
3 BAILEY: Excuse me? Are you talking to me?
4 PATRICK: You are smelling strong today, Bailey Richards.
5 BAILEY: Patrick, don't you mean, I smell pretty?
6 PATRICK: No, but pretty strong is what I say. Woo wee!
7 BAILEY: Woo wee?
8 PATRICK: Oh, it's just a saying that I have. Like when we
9   passed a dead skunk ... *woo wee!* Or when you smell
10   pretty strong today ... *woo wee!*
11 BAILEY: You're comparing me to a skunk?
12 PATRICK: A sweet-smelling skunk.
13 BAILEY: Patrick, you are so mean. You know that's not true.
14   I just put on a little extra perfume this morning
15   because ...
16 PATRICK: A *little* extra? Are you sure you didn't bathe in
17   your toilet?
18 BAILEY: Excuse me?
19 PATRICK: You know ... bathe in that E.D. toilet?
20 BAILEY: That's Eau De Toilette, Patrick. You're such an
21   idiot. And ... I just splashed on a little extra here ...
22   *(Touches her neck.)* And a little extra there ... *(Touches*
23   *her wrists.)*
24 PATRICK: Don't you mean you splashed on half a bottle?
25 BAILEY: I think your nose is too sensitive.
26 PATRICK: *(Waving his hand in front of his face)* No, I don't
27   think so. I'm sorry, Bailey, but I could smell you
28   coming.
29 BAILEY: Stop exaggerating.

1   PATRICK: I'm not! I swear! So tell me, why did you put on

2   all the extra E.D. Toilet?

3   BAILEY: *(Glares at him.)* Because I have a lunch date with

4   Bryan and I wanted him to think I smelled pretty.

5   PATRICK: Well, he'll think you smell pretty strong. But

6   maybe he'll like it. *(Waves his hand in front of his face.)*

7   Woo wee! Let's hope so.

8   BAILEY: Of course he will. Boys like the smell of perfume.

9   At least *most* boys do.

10   PATRICK: Well, hopefully Bryan will have a cold.

11   BAILEY: Have a cold? Why do you say that?

12   PATRICK: So you don't knock him over with your attempt

13   to smell pretty. Woo wee!

14   BAILEY: Patrick, why don't you and your extra-sensitive

15   nose find somewhere else to wait for the bell to ring?

16   Bryan is meeting me here in a few minutes and I

17   don't want you saying anything stupid in front of

18   him.

19   PATRICK: Bailey, I'm sorry for being honest. And no, I

20   don't have an extra-sensitive nose. Because last week,

21   Phil ate these super strong red onions on his burger

22   then asked if his breath smelled OK ...

23   BAILEY: He asked you to smell his breath?

24   PATRICK: Yeah. He did this. *(Breathes out on BAILEY.)*

25   Then he said, "Tell me if my breath stinks." And I was

26   like no. Seems fine to me. Well, after school, Phil

27   went to give Naida a good-bye kiss and he said she did

28   this ... *(Imitates her.)* "Oh my gosh! Get away from me!

29   You've been eating onions. Stay away. Yuck!" Well, I

30   never even smelled the onions on Phil's breath. But

31   you ...wow ... that E.D. Toilet water stuff is awfully

32   overpowering.

33   BAILEY: Patrick, you're just saying that to be mean. And I

34   don't know why.

35   PATRICK: Can't you smell it?

1   **BAILEY:** *(Smells her wrist.)* **It's not overpowering.**

2   **PATRICK: Really?** *(Waves his arms in the air.)* **Well, I can**

3   **smell it everywhere. In fact, I'm sure that by now,**

4   **just standing here next to you, I smell like a stinkin'**

5   **girl.** *(Steps away.)* **Yeah, I think I better stand over**

6   **here.**

7   **BAILEY: You can't smell me from over there.**

8   **PATRICK: Let me get a little further away ...** *(Moves back.)*

9   **That's better. Now, you walk this way and I'll tell you**

10 **when I can smell your toilet water.**

11 **BAILEY: It's perfume, Patrick!**

12 **PATRICK: OK, OK. So walk over here and we'll test this**

13   **out one more time. Just to make sure.** *(BAILEY takes a*

14   *few steps toward PATRICK.)*

15 **PATRICK: *Woo wee!* I can already smell you from here.**

16 *(BAILEY screams and starts to exit.)*

17 **PATRICK: Hey, where are you going?**

18 **BAILEY:** *(Stops and turns to him.)* **I'm going home to take a**

19   **shower.**

20 **PATRICK: But what about Bryan? Lunch date?**

21 **BAILEY: Tell him I can't make it.** *(Exits.)*

22 **PATRICK: *Woo wee!* I can still smell her.** *(Waves his arms in*

23   *the air.)* **I need some air freshener. Man, I'm gonna be**

24   **smelling like a dang girl.** *(Exits.)*

51. Lunch Order

CAST: MRS. WARREN, CARSON
PROPS: Textbook, cell phone
SETTING: Classroom

1   *(At rise, CARSON hides behind a textbook, talking quietly*
2   *on his cell phone. MRS. WARREN walks over to his desk*
3   *and stands over him for a moment before saying*
4   *anything.)*
5   **MRS. WARREN: Mr. Jones.**
6   **CARSON:** *(Into his cell phone)* **Hold on.** *(Lowers his book and*
7   *looks at MRS. WARREN.)* **Yes, ma'am?**
8   **MRS. WARREN: Are you talking on your cell phone?**
9   **CARSON: Who me?**
10   **MRS. WARREN: Yes, you. Hand it over.** *(Holds out her hand.)*
11   **CARSON:** *(Hands her the phone.)* **I'm sorry, Mrs. Warren.**
12   **MRS. WARREN:** *(Into the phone)* **Who is this? Who?** *(Looks at*
13   *CARSON.)* **You were ordering pizza?** *(Into phone)* **I don't**
14   **know if he wants to cut the mushrooms.**
15   **CARSON: Yes! Tell him to cut the mushrooms. And the**
16   **green peppers. And can you tell him I want to add**
17   **jalapeños and pineapple? And that was the stuffed**
18   **crust pizza, if he didn't get that.**
19   **MRS. WARREN:** *(Into the phone)* **He'll have to call you back.**
20   **What? Yes. He wants to cut the mushrooms. Listen**
21   **here, Mr. Pizza Man, Carson is at school right now and**
22   **talking on the cell phone is strictly prohibited unless**
23   **it's an emergency.**
24   **CARSON:** *(Under his breath)* **It was an emergency.**
25   **MRS. WARREN:** *(Into the phone)* **What? Yes, I think he**
26   **wanted to cut the green peppers, too.**
27   **CARSON: I did. Thank you.**
28   **MRS. WARREN:** *(Into the phone)* **But the point is, Mr. Pizza**

1   Man, Carson is sitting in American history and he
2   has no business placing a pizza order in my
3   classroom. What? *(Yells.)* Yes, I think he said stuffed
4   crust!
5 CARSON: I did.
6 MRS. WARREN: *(Into the phone)* And what were you going
7   to do? Deliver pizza to the school between classes?
8   Oh, really?
9 CARSON: We order pizza and eat them in the drama
10   room. Mr. Shields doesn't care.
11 MRS. WARREN: *(Into the phone)* Excuse me? I don't know,
12   Mr. Pizza Man. I don't recall what he wanted to add.
13 CARSON: Jalapeños and pineapple. Please.
14 MRS. WARREN: *(Into the phone)* Did you hear that? *(Yells.)*
15   Jalapeños and pineapple! Please!
16 CARSON: Thank you, Mrs. Warren. My mouth is already
17   watering.
18 MRS. WARREN: *(Into the phone)* So don't you think it'd be
19   wise to tell students that pizza orders should only be
20   placed during lunch hour? Yes, I realize you need
21   time to make it for lunch, but my students need to be
22   paying attention during my class. What? *(To*
23   *CARSON)* Did you want onions?
24 CARSON: Yes. Lots.
25 MRS. WARREN: *(Into the phone)* Good. I'm glad you heard
26   that. Well, I don't know if that's delivery or take out.
27   *(Looks at CARSON.)*
28 CARSON: Delivery, please. Drama room.
29 MRS. WARREN: *(Into the phone)* Yes, I'm glad you heard
30   that, too. What? Well, I don't know if it's cash or
31   credit card.
32 CARSON: Cash.
33 MRS. WARREN: *(Into the phone)* Cash. And your special is
34   what? Two for one? Today only?
35 CARSON: Yes! Give me two for one today.

1 **MRS. WARREN:** *(Into the phone)* **Yes. Two for one.**
2 **CARSON: Yes!**
3 **MRS. WARREN:** *(Into the phone)* **But that second pizza**
4   **needs to be delivered to Room two-oh-eight. And I do**
5   **not want mushrooms on mine.**
6 **CARSON: What?**
7 **MRS. WARREN: Yes, I'll be receiving the free pizza. That's**
8   **right. Room two-oh-eight.** *(Laughs.)* **Yes, yes, that's**
9   **fine.** *(Hangs up the phone.)* **Our pizzas will be here**
10   **soon.**
11 **CARSON: Our pizzas?**
12 **MRS. WARREN:** *(Smiles.)* **That's right.**
13 **CARSON: So you're not mad?**
14 **MRS. WARREN: I am mad, but I'm hungry and I don't**
15   **want to eat that stinking cafeteria food one more day.**
16   **Now, open your history book to chapter thirteen and**
17   **read.**
18 **CARSON: Yes, ma'am.**
19 **MRS. WARREN: And by the way, you'll be the one to tip the**
20   **delivery driver. Not me.**
21 **CARSON: Yes, ma'am.**
22 **MRS. WARREN: Now, read!** *(CARSON reads.)* **Yes, my**
23   **mouth is watering already. I love pizza.**

52. A Chance

CAST: CHASE, LESLIE
SETTING: Classroom

1 CHASE: So, what do you say?
2 LESLIE: I'll think about it.
3 CHASE: You mean you'll actually consider it?
4 LESLIE: Yes. I'll let you know.
5 CHASE: When? Today?
6 LESLIE: Can I text you my answer?
7 CHASE: Of course. Thank you!
8 LESLIE: For what?
9 CHASE: For thinking about it. For not immediately saying
10   no. For giving me a chance.
11 LESLIE: OK.
12 CHASE: Would you say it's a fifty-fifty chance?
13 LESLIE: I guess.
14 CHASE: That's great. I'll take it. I have a fifty percent chance
15   that you'll say yes.
16 LESLIE: And a fifty percent chance I'll say no.
17 CHASE: But you don't want to say no right now, do you?
18 LESLIE: Chase, I said I'd think about it.
19 CHASE: And take all the time you want. But could you give
20   me your answer by the end of the day? Because if you
21   say no, I need to figure out who else to invite.
22 LESLIE: So soon?
23 CHASE: Well I can't go to the prom alone, can I?
24 LESLIE: You could. Some people have more fun going with
25   a group of friends instead of having a date.
26 CHASE: Well, all my friends have dates, so ...
27 LESLIE: So you want a date, too.
28 CHASE: Yes, but not just any date. I want you for my date.
29 LESLIE: Ah ... that's sweet. And like I said, I'll think about it.

1   **CHASE: And text me your answer?**

2   **LESLIE: By the end of the day.**

3   **CHASE: Perfect!**

4   **LESLIE: OK. See ya.**

5   **CHASE: Wait!** *(She stops.)* **Do you know which way you're**

6   **leaning? A little this way ... yes ... or a little that way ...**

7   **no?**

8   **LESLIE: I'm in the middle.**

9   **CHASE: Well, is there anything I could do to persuade you**

10   **to lean toward a yes?**

11   **LESLIE: I don't think so. Like I said, I need to think about**

12   **it.**

13   **CHASE: So, do you have two or three other guys you're**

14   **thinking about going with, too?**

15   **LESLIE: I didn't say that.**

16   **CHASE: I'm not the first person to ask you to the prom,**

17   **am I?**

18   **LESLIE: The seventh.**

19   **CHASE: The seventh?!**

20   **LESLIE: And I haven't decided who I want to go with yet.**

21   **But I'm going to make up my mind today.**

22   **CHASE: Seven?**

23   **LESLIE: Yes. Seven invites.**

24   **CHASE: So really, instead of having a fifty-fifty chance, I**

25   **have a one in seven chance.**

26   **LESLIE: I guess you could say that.**

27   **CHASE: These odds are not looking so good anymore.**

28   **LESLIE: I'll text you my answer later, OK?**

29   **CHASE: Wait! Tell me. What do you like in a guy? Tell me**

30   **the top five things.**

31   **LESLIE: Well, he has to be cute.**

32   **CHASE: Check! Look right here. I'm cute.**

33   **LESLIE: He has to have a good sense of humor. You know,**

34   **fun to be around.**

35   **CHASE: Cute and fun. So far, so good! Next.**

1 LESLIE: Romantic.
2 CHASE: Darling, I love the way the artificial light brings
3   out the color of your eyes. See, I was funny *and*
4   romantic.
5 LESLIE: And I like guys who are intelligent.
6 CHASE: And who aced their algebra test today? That
7   would be me. What else?
8 LESLIE: Trustworthy.
9 CHASE: Baby, I'm as loyal and trustworthy as they come.
10   You choose me and I'm yours for life.
11 LESLIE: How about you're mine just for the prom?
12 CHASE: OK, OK, that works, too.
13 LESLIE: So anyway, I'll text you my answer later today.
14 CHASE: Wait! One more thing. *(She stops.)* You're not just
15   saying you'll think about it so you don't have to tell
16   me no to my face, are you?
17 LESLIE: No.
18 CHASE: No you don't want to go with me or no you're not
19   just saying you'll think about it so you don't have to
20   look in my eyes when you break my heart?
21 LESLIE: No!
22 CHASE: No what?
23 LESLIE: No ... I don't know! I'm confused.
24 CHASE: If you want to say no, just go ahead and do it.
25 LESLIE: Chase, I said I'd think about it.
26 CHASE: You will?
27 LESLIE: Yes.
28 CHASE: Yes?
29 LESLIE: Yes.
30 CHASE: Yes? You picked me to take you to prom?
31 LESLIE: No! Chase, I've got to think about it. I'll text you.
32 CHASE: So would you say it's a one in seven chance or
33   more like a fifty-fifty chance?
34 LESLIE: I'd just say there's a chance.
35 CHASE: OK, OK, I'll take that. And you'll text me by the

1   **end of the day?**

2   **LESLIE:** *(As she exits.)* **Yes!**

3   **CHASE: Hey, the odds are better than winning the lottery.**

4   **One in seven, one in millions ... I'll take my chance.**

53. Bad Student

CAST: MRS. SMITH, MIGUEL
PROPS: Student desk
SETTING: Hallway

1　*(At rise, MIGUEL, a student, sits at his desk. After a*
2　*moment, he waves his hand in the air and continues until*
3　*MRS. SMITH, the teacher, notices him.)*
4　**MRS. SMITH: Yes?**
5　**MIGUEL: I'm sorry.**
6　**MRS. SMITH: OK.**
7　**MIGUEL: Am I forgiven?**
8　**MRS. SMITH: Sure.**
9　**MIGUEL:** *(Stands.)* **Thank you.**
10　**MRS. SMITH: Sit.** *(MIGUEL sits.)* **But you're not going**
11　　**anywhere until the end of the day.**
12　**MIGUEL: I have to sit here all day?**
13　**MRS. SMITH: Yes. You can do your schoolwork here, eat**
14　　**your lunch here, watch students walk to their next**
15　　**classes, be embarrassed, cry, whine, complain ...**
16　　**whatever ... but you are stuck here with me all day. Fun,**
17　　**isn't it?**
18　**MIGUEL: Do you like being a prison guard?**
19　**MRS. SMITH: Hallway monitor slash teacher slash prison**
20　　**guard ... yes. The teachers have had enough of your fun**
21　　**and games in their classes, so today you're going to pay.**
22　**MIGUEL: But I'm sorry.**
23　**MRS. SMITH: I bet you are. And you're also an example to**
24　　**the other students of what can happen to them if they**
25　　**continually misbehave in class.**
26　**MIGUEL: Sit in a desk in the hallway to be laughed at?**
27　**MRS. SMITH: Yes. All day long. Because you, Miguel, are a**
28　　**bad student. A very, very bad student.**

1   MIGUEL: Who's ever heard of making a kid sit in the
2   hallway? How can I learn out here?
3   MRS. SMITH: It's called punishment. Fun, isn't it?
4   MIGUEL: No! And it's boring.
5   MRS. SMITH: Oh, well.
6   MIGUEL: *(After a pause, he taps his finger on his desk as*
7   *if playing the drums.)* **Da-dum, da-dum, da, da, da,**
8   **dum ...**
9   MRS. SMITH: Stop it. Your desk is not a drum set.
10   MIGUEL: But I'm bored.
11   MRS. SMITH: Read your history book.
12   MIGUEL: *(Reads for a minute.)* **I'm lonely out here.**
13   MRS. SMITH: Me too.
14   MIGUEL: At least we have each other, huh?
15   MRS. SMITH: Hush! Read your book.
16   MIGUEL: Did you really intend to grow up to be a hallway
17   monitor?
18   MRS. SMITH: I'm a teacher.
19   MIGUEL: Doesn't look like it today.
20   MRS. SMITH: Who's periodically assigned to hallway duty.
21   To control the little devils such as yourself who have
22   no understanding of respect.
23   MIGUEL: I said I was sorry.
24   MRS. SMTIH: Whatever.
25   MIGUEL: *(After a pause)* And you really wanted to grow up
26   to be a teacher?
27   MRS. SMITH: Yes.
28   MIGUEL: Why?
29   MRS. SMITH: Right now I'm wondering that myself.
30   MIGUEL: Sounds like we're both having a bad day. *(Pounds*
31   *his head on the desk.)* I hate my life. I hate my life.
32   MRS. SMITH: Stop that.
33   MIGUEL: Doesn't it make you want to pound your head on
34   the wall? Why don't you do it? It might make you feel
35   better.

1   MRS. SMITH: *(Raises her hand to him.)* **What I'd like to do**
2   **is pound something else.**
3   MIGUEL: *(Pulls away.)* **Don't hit me. Please don't hit me!**
4   MRS. SMITH: **Stop it! I wasn't going to. I just want to.**
5   MIGUEL: **Oh. OK.**
6   MRS. SMITH: **Oh, I need a cup of coffee.**
7   MIGUEL: **Me too. Hey, why don't you go to the teachers'**
8   **lounge and get some? Who would know?**
9   MRS. SMITH: **Don't tempt me. But I can't leave you here**
10   **alone.**
11   MIGUEL: **Then take me with you. Please. Take me with**
12   **you! Let's go get some coffee. It's the only way you**
13   **and I are going to get through this horrid, boring,**
14   **never-ending day. And I won't tell. Oh, coffee ... I can**
15   **smell you! That wonderful aroma. I can taste you on**
16   **my lips. The energy I derive from you ... Hey, I won't**
17   **tell!**
18   MRS. SMITH: **You promise?**
19   MIGUEL: *(Jumps up.)* **I promise.**
20   MRS. SMITH: **Let's hurry. We go in, we go out, and don't**
21   **speak to anyone or make any noises, do you hear me?**
22   MIGUEL: **Yes, ma'am.** *(As they start off)* **I take mine with**
23   **cream and sugar.**
24   MRS. SMITH: **You're getting water.**
25   MIGUEL: **Water? That's it?**
26   MRS. SMITH: **That's it.**
27   MIGUEL: **Man, this is prison.**
28   MRS. SMITH: **That's right and don't forget it.**
29   MIGUEL: **I'm really sorry, Mrs. Smith. I guess I really am**
30   **a bad student.**
31   MRS. SMITH: **Yes you are.**
32   MIGUEL: **Talking during class, making paper airplanes,**
33   **opening cans of sardines, pretending to be a foreign**
34   **exchange student, stealing a grade book and**
35   **changing the grades ...** *(Suddenly laughs out loud.)*

1   **And it was all great!** *(After MRS. SMITH gives him a*
2   *dirty look.)* **Yes, I'm a very bad student. A very, very**
3   **bad student. Are you sure I can't have some coffee?**
4   **Please?** *(MRS. SMITH shakes her head.)*

54. Short Memory

CAST: JORDAN, ALLISON
SETTING: Living room

1   *(At rise, JORDAN is looking at a piece of tape that is*
2   *wrapped around his finger. ALLISON, his sister, enters*
3   *the room.)*
4 JORDAN: Man!
5 ALLISON: What's wrong, big brother?
6 JORDAN: *(Showing her his finger)* This.
7 ALLISON: What happened? Did you cut yourself?
8 JORDAN: No. I put this tape on my finger to remind me of
9   something I needed to do.
10 ALLISON: Oh, what's that?
11 JORDAN: I can't remember.
12 ALLISON: You're telling me that you put tape on your finger
13   to remember something and now you can't remember
14   whatever it was you wanted to remember?
15 JORDAN: Yes. How stupid is that?
16 ALLISON: Pretty stupid, Jordan.
17 JORDAN: Thanks, Allison.
18 ALLISON: I'm teasing. Let me help you remember.
19 JORDAN: I've been trying to do that! It's not working.
20 ALLISON: Homework assignment?
21 JORDAN: All my homework has been completed.
22 ALLISON: Take out the garbage?
23 JORDAN: Done.
24 ALLISON: Sweep the leaves outside that you've been
25   warned about doing?
26 JORDAN: Done.
27 ALLISON: Call someone?
28 JORDAN: Who?
29 ALLISON: I don't know. That's for you to remember.

1   JORDAN: I don't think that's it.

2   ALLISON: Feed the dog?

3   JORDAN: Did that.

4   ALLISON: Give the dog water.

5   JORDAN: Did that, too.

6   ALLISON: Meet someone somewhere?

7   JORDAN: Who and where?

8   ALLISON: I don't know, Jordan? I'm just trying to help jog

9   your memory.

10 JORDAN: I don't think that's it, but keep trying.

11 ALLISON: *(Deep breath)* I'm running out of ideas. Let's see

12   ... Pick a date for the homecoming dance?

13 JORDAN: Nope. Got one.

14 ALLISON: I know! Watch some sporting event on TV?

15 JORDAN: That's not it.

16 ALLISON: Pick up something from the store?

17 JORDAN: What?

18 ALLISON: I don't know, Jordan. It's your stuff.

19 JORDAN: That's not it.

20 ALLISON: Return a movie you rented?

21 JORDAN: Haven't rented any lately.

22 ALLISON: Visit someone in the hospital?

23 JORDAN: Who?

24 ALLISON: I don't know, Jordan. It's your sick friend.

25 JORDAN: But I don't have a sick friend in the hospital. At

26   least I don't think I do.

27 ALLISON: Take something out of the oven?

28 JORDAN: No. I'd use a kitchen timer if I cooked and I

29   rarely do that.

30 ALLISON: Return something you borrowed from

31   someone?

32 JORDAN: What and to who?

33 ALLISON: I don't know, Jordan! You borrowed it!

34 JORDAN: No. I haven't borrowed anything lately. At least I

35   don't think I have.

1 ALLISON: Pay someone back some money you borrowed?
2 JORDAN: To who?
3 ALLISON: I don't know! You borrowed the money.
4 JORDAN: The only person I've borrowed money from is
5   Mom and I don't have any money to pay her back.
6 ALLISON: Revenge?
7 JORDAN: Against Mom?
8 ALLISON: No! Of course not. Against your enemy.
9 JORDAN: Who's my enemy?
10 ALLISON: I don't know, Jordan. You tell me.
11 JORDAN: But I don't have an enemy.
12 ALLISON: Jordan, I'm sorry, but I'm running out of ideas.
13 JORDAN: Try a few more, Allison. Please! *(Holds up finger.)*
14   Because this is driving me crazy.
15 ALLISON: All right. I'll try. Take your vitamin?
16 JORDAN: Did that this morning.
17 ALLISON: Feed the fish?
18 JORDAN: Did that.
19 ALLISON: Brush your teeth?
20 JORDAN: Allison, I don't need to put a reminder on my
21   finger to brush my teeth.
22 ALLISON: Yeah, right. Mom is always reminding you to
23   brush your teeth.
24 JORDAN: That's not what this is about. *(Holds up his*
25   *finger.)*
26 ALLISON: Then what's it for?
27 JORDAN: I can't remember.
28 ALLISON: Well, that's dumb.
29 JORDAN: Thank you.
30 ALLISON: Next time, why don't you try writing yourself a
31   note instead?
32 JORDAN: Believe me, I will. But that doesn't help me right
33   now. What was so important?
34 ALLISON: My birthday?
35 JORDAN: That's not important. *(ALLISON glares at him.)*

1   And it's not until next month. And how could I forget
2   it when you remind everyone for weeks ahead of
3   time. *(Sounding like a girl)* "Next week is my birthday.
4   Oh! I wonder what I'm going to get! Oh! I wonder if
5   someone's going to throw me a surprise party?"
6 ALLISON: Oh, shut up. But I do know one thing.
7 JORDAN: What?
8 ALLISON: When you finally remember what you forgot to
9   do, it'll be too late.
10 JORDAN: Why do you say that?
11 ALLISON: Because if you went to the trouble to put a piece
12   of tape on your finger, it's probably something very
13   important. Like studying for a test tomorrow. Then
14   you'll be sitting in class, say history, staring at your
15   finger, still wondering what you were supposed to
16   remember, then Mr. Shields will pass out the history
17   exam and then you'll be like, "Ah, man! Now I
18   remember. I was supposed to study for this exam."
19   And then you'll be like, "Oh, no!" Because then it'll be
20   too late.
21 JORDAN: Allison, for your information, I don't have any
22   tests tomorrow.
23 ALLISON: Well, that's good. Was it to remind you to show
24   up at the pep rally tomorrow? To see your little sister
25   cheer on the Rams?
26 JORDAN: That's it! I remembered!
27 ALLISON: *(Surprised)* That was it? I'm touched, Jordan.
28 JORDAN: No, it was to remind me to remind you that you
29   need to pick up your cheerleading uniform from the
30   cleaners. They called the house.
31 ALLISON: What? They called?
32 JORDAN: I guess Mom forgot to pick up your uniform this
33   afternoon and they're closed for some sort of repairs
34   tomorrow so they wanted to make sure you picked up
35   your uniform by the end of the day.

1   **ALLISON: Oh my gosh! My cheerleading uniform! I need**
2   **it for the pep rally in the morning! What time do they**
3   **close?**
4   **JORDAN: Five thirty.**
5   **ALLISON: And what time is it?**
6   **JORDAN:** *(Looks at his watch.)* **Six-forty-five. When they**
7   **called they said they'd be closing in an hour.** *(Holds*
8   *up his finger.)* **I remembered. Yeah!**
9   **ALLISON:** *(Runs off screaming.)* **Call Mom and tell her I**
10   **might be going to jail for breaking and entering the**
11   **cleaners.**
12   **JORDAN: OK.** *(Holds up his finger.)* **That is, if I can**
13   **remember.**

55. Christmas Excitement

CAST: NATALIE, AIDEN
SETTING: The city pool

1 NATALIE: *(Sings.)* "Jingle bells, jingle bells, jingle all the
2   way ... "
3 AIDEN: Natalie, why are you singing that song? It's like a
4   hundred degrees outside and not even close to
5   Christmas.
6 NATALIE: Because I love Christmas. I love everything about
7   it. *(Sings.)* "Dashing through the snow, in a one horse
8   open sleigh ... "
9 AIDEN: If you love Christmas so much, do you want to get
10   started early?
11 NATALIE: What do you mean?
12 AIDEN: On my Christmas list. I'll start it for you.
13 NATALIE: Give it to me in a few months because I'm broke
14   right now. But in the meantime ... *(Sings.)* "I'll be home
15   for Christmas, you can plan on me. Please have snow
16   and mistletoe, and presents on the tree ... "
17 AIDEN: Natalie, at this rate, you're going to be sick of
18   Christmas by the time it's here.
19 NATALIE: Never! I love Christmas. The smells, the sounds,
20   the excitement ...
21 AIDEN: Well, you've got awhile to wait. Make that six
22   months.
23 NATALIE: You know, Aiden, I wish my mom would let us
24   leave the Christmas tree up all year long.
25 AIDEN: My mom can't wait to take it down after we've
26   opened the presents.
27 NATALIE: My mom, too, but wouldn't it be more fun to leave
28   it up all year long?
29 AIDEN: Then where's the excitement in putting up the tree?

1   And what if it's a real tree? It's going to die. Pine
2   needles everywhere.
3 NATALIE: Good point. Oh well, it was just a thought.
4   *(Sings.)* "Frosty the snowman was a jolly happy soul,
5   with a corncob pipe and a button nose, and two eyes
6   made out of coal ... " Don't you just love that song?
7 AIDEN: It's OK. And thank you, but I think I've had
8   enough of Christmas for now.
9 NATALIE: Enough of Christmas? Aiden, how can you say
10   that?
11 AIDEN: Natalie, Christmas is months away, we're sitting
12   here at the city pool and it's like a hundred degrees
13   outside. I'd rather think about jumping off the
14   diving board or floating in the pool while working on
15   my tan.
16 NATALIE: While thinking about what you want for
17   Christmas?
18 AIDEN: It's too far away to think about that.
19 NATALIE: A new bike?
20 AIDEN: A new car would be better.
21 NATALIE: New games for your Xbox?
22 AIDEN: Yeah, I could go for that.
23 NATALIE: New laptop?
24 AIDEN: iPad! Yeah, I'd take one of those. Maybe I should
25   go ahead and start my Christmas list so Mom could
26   get an early start on it.
27 NATALIE: Good idea.
28 AIDEN: Mom always likes me to give her my Christmas
29   wish list early so she can start looking for those great
30   deals at the stores. So maybe this year I'll give it to
31   her really early. Say six months early.
32 NATALIE: And keep adding to it during the year.
33 AIDEN: Yeah! I want this, and this, and this, and ... You
34   know, I do like Christmas.
35 NATALIE: I love Christmas!

1   AIDEN: I love Christmas presents!

2   NATALIE: The smells, the sounds ... the excitement!

3   AIDEN: Opening gifts.

4   NATALIE: Shopping.

5   AIDEN: Seeing what Santa brought me.

6   NATALIE: The decorations, the lights, the tinsel, wrapping

7   paper, bows ...

8   AIDEN: Presents! All for me.

9   NATALIE: Leaving cookies out for Santa even if I don't

10   believe he's really real, but secretly hoping he is ...

11 AIDEN: Not being able to sleep. Can't wait for morning so

12   I can open my presents.

13 NATALIE: Running into the living room!

14 AIDEN: Oh, yes! Santa you outdid yourself this year!

15   Presents everywhere. All for me.

16 NATALIE: *(As if handing him a gift)* For you.

17 AIDEN: *(As if taking the gift)* Thank you! It's just what I

18   wanted.

19 NATALIE: See, don't you love Christmas?

20 AIDEN: I do! I love it! And I can't wait. And tonight I'm

21   going to start on my Christmas list.

22 NATALIE: *(Sings.)* "Jingle bells, jingle bells, jingle all the

23   way ... "

24 AIDEN: So what if it's a hundred degrees outside. *(Sings.)*

25   "Jingle bells, jingle bells, jingle all the way ... "

56. Dumped

CAST: AMBER, DEVIN
SETTING: School hallway

1 AMBER: Let's get this straight. I broke up with you.
2 DEVIN: Mutual decision.
3 AMBER: No. I dumped you.
4 DEVIN: Incorrect. I suggested we go our separate ways.
5 AMBER: Devin, you are so confused right now.
6 DEVIN: No, Amber. You're just trying to come up with a
7   version that suits you so you can look good in the end.
8 AMBER: No. Let's get this straight. I am the dump-er and you
9   are dumped.
10 DEVIN: Don't you mean I was the first one who hinted that
11   it wasn't working out for me?
12 AMBER: Well, it wasn't working out for me, either. That's
13   why I dumped you.
14 DEVIN: I thought we agreed to call it quits.
15 AMBER: I didn't agree to anything.
16 DEVIN: You wanted to stay together?
17 AMBER: I didn't say that.
18 DEVIN: And try to make something work that obviously
19   wasn't?
20 AMBER: I was only letting it drag on because I hate hurting
21   other people's feelings. Because I understand, Devin,
22   that being dumped by your girlfriend can be very
23   painful. Do you need a hug?
24 DEVIN: I'm not hurt.
25 AMBER: Yes you are.
26 DEVIN: No. More like relieved that it's over.
27 AMBER: Then we agree it was the right decision.
28 DEVIN: I'll agree with that. And we can now both go our
29   separate ways.

1   AMBER: I'm thrilled to go our separate ways!

2   DEVIN: It was good while it lasted, but it came to an end.

3   AMBER: Thank goodness it came to an end. Hallelujah.

4   DEVIN: And all that said, we came to the mutual decision

5   to break up.

6   AMBER: No! I broke up with you. You just can't face the

7   truth — I'm the dump-er and you are dumped.

8   DEVIN: Is that what we are going to tell our friends? You

9   dumped me?

10 AMBER: I'm sorry, Devin, but it's true. Do you need a hug?

11   Here, I'll give you one.

12 DEVIN: Stop! You are only saying you dumped me after I

13   confronted you and said it wasn't working out for me

14   anymore. Then your eyes swelled up with tears, and —

15 AMBER: They did not! I wouldn't cry over you.

16 DEVIN: And then you said we could work it out. And that

17   we were perfect for one another.

18 AMBER: Such an exaggeration! Or shall I say, such an

19   imagination that you have.

20 DEVIN: And then I apologized and said I was sorry it

21   didn't feel right to me anymore.

22 AMBER: I thought you said it didn't feel right for us to

23   part.

24 DEVIN: As enemies. I meant, I didn't want us to part as

25   enemies.

26 AMBER: You're not going to accept the truth are you? I

27   broke up with you and you can't stand it.

28 DEVIN: All right, fine!

29 AMBER: Fine?

30 DEVIN: If you insist on telling our friends that you

31   dumped me, fine.

32 AMBER: No, no, we'll do it your way. Even though your

33   story is out of nowhere. We'll tell our friends that you

34   are a cold, heartless person who broke my heart.

35   Then you just move right along because I'm sure I'll

1   receive plenty of sympathy from our friends.

2   DEVIN: What? Cold and heartless?

3   AMBER: Cold and heartless as they come!

4   DEVIN: No, wait. I didn't break up with you. You broke up

5   with me! Remember? I don't want to be deemed as

6   the mean person here.

7   AMBER: No, it's final. I accept the fact that you broke up

8   with me, Devin. Yes, you are quite the cold and

9   heartless person. Wait until our friends hear. I can

10   surely play the poor, dumped, pitiful, heartbroken

11   person for quite some time. All the guys will want to

12   give me hugs. *(Glares at him.)* But there will be no

13   hugs for you! *(Gently)* But for me ... yes, I do need a

14   hug. *(Begins to cry as she exits.)* Hey, guys! Wait till you

15   hear what Devin did to me.

57. Schedule Change

CAST: BEN, MRS. SIMMS
PROPS: Schedule, notebook
SETTING: School office

1 (At rise, BEN has entered the school office and
2 approaches MRS. SIMMS, an office worker.)
3 BEN: I need to change my schedule.
4 MRS. SIMMS: (Looks at his schedule.) Why? What's wrong
5 with it?
6 BEN: They put me in choir.
7 MRS. SIMMS: That's because you signed up for choir.
8 BEN: No I didn't. I can promise you that.
9 MRS. SIMMS: Then let me check on this. (Flips through a
10 notebook.) Oh yes. You were one of the lucky ones.
11 BEN: What do you mean? *One of the lucky ones?*
12 MRS. SIMMS: Who was randomly picked to participate in
13 choir this year.
14 BEN: What?!
15 MRS. SIMMS: You see, Ben, hardly anyone signed up for
16 choir this year and we needed students in the class.
17 Because without students, the school can't have a
18 choir. Which would mean no yuletide follies, spring
19 concert, patriotic program, and so on. So therefore we
20 let our computer randomly pick fifty extra students to
21 enroll in choir this year. (Smiles at him.) Congratulations.
22 BEN: No, no! You've got to change my schedule, Mrs. Simms.
23 I don't want to be in choir.
24 MRS. SIMMS: I'm sorry, Ben, but it's final. But I can tell you
25 that if you decide choir is not your thing, you won't be
26 forced to take it again next year.
27 BEN: Are you seriously telling me that you're forcing me to
28 participate in choir this year?

1   MRS. SIMMS: Yes. *(Smiles.)* **Congratulations.**

2   BEN: No! I can't be in choir.

3   MRS. SIMMS: Yes, you will. For the better of our school.

4   BEN: But I hate singing.

5   MRS. SIMMS: Then you'll learn to like it. The patriotic
6   program is next month. And I will be there. Front
7   row. As I'm sure your parents will be too.

8   BEN: But you don't understand. I can't sing!

9   MRS. SIMMS: Hogwash. Everyone can sing.

10 BEN: Not me. I can't. I really can't.

11 MRS. SIMMS: If you can talk, you can sing.

12 BEN: Not me.

13 MRS. SIMMS: Do this. "La, la, la, la, la ... "

14 BEN: "La, la, la, la, la ... "

15 MRS. SIMMS: See there. You can sing.

16 BEN: No, I can't! If anyone could ruin a patriotic song, that
17   would be me.

18 MRS. SIMMS: Hogwash! You'll blend in with all the
19   others.

20 BEN: I doubt that. Look, Mrs. Simms, I'm telling you, your
21   computer picked the wrong person.

22 MRS. SIMMS: Nice try, Ben, but you're stuck. No schedule
23   changes.

24 BEN: No! Please! I'm begging you. I need my schedule
25   changed now. Please.

26 MRS. SIMMS: Begging won't help.

27 BEN: Will singing help?

28 MRS. SIMMS: What?

29 BEN: If you heard me sing, would that help?

30 MRS. SIMMS: Why would that help?

31 BEN: Because then you could hear how horrible I sound.

32 MRS. SIMMS: You can't be that horrible.

33 BEN: Believe me, I am.

34 MRS. SIMMS: OK, let's hear it then. And no faking to
35   sound bad. I want to hear your true singing voice.

1 BEN: Yes ma'am. But I'm warning you, I'm bad.

2 MRS. SIMMS: Go ahead.

3 BEN: What do you want me to sing?

4 MRS. SIMMS: How about a patriotic song?

5 BEN: OK. *(Clears his throat, then sings very badly.)* "Oh

6   beautiful for spacious skies, For amber waves of

7   grain, For purple mountain majesties, Above the

8   fruited plain, America! America! God shed his grace

9   on thee!"

10 MRS. SIMMS: Stop!

11 BEN: It was bad, wasn't it?

12 MRS. SIMMS: Try a different song. Maybe that will help.

13 BEN: *(Sings badly.)* "My country 'tis of thee, Sweet land of

14   liberty, Of thee I sing, Land where my fathers died,

15   Land of the Pilgrims' pride – "

16 MRS. SIMMS: Stop!

17 BEN: It was bad, wasn't it?

18 MRS. SIMMS: Horrible! Absolutely horrible. Gut-

19   wrenching! The most painful thing I've ever heard in

20   my life.

21 BEN: Told you so. I tried to warn you.

22 MRS. SIMMS: *(Writes on his schedule, then hands it to him.)*

23   Choir is out for you. Here you go. *(Hands him the*

24   *schedule.)* I've put you in auto mechanics instead.

25 BEN: Thank you. Thank you. Thank you!

26 MRS. SIMMS: Oh, and Ben ...

27 BEN: Yes ma'am?

28 MRS. SIMMS: Save your singing for the shower.

29 BEN: Yes ma'am!

58. Superhero

CAST: KELLY, SCOTT
PROPS: Cape for Scott to wear
SETTING: Outside Scott's house

1   *(At rise, KELLY enters and finds SCOTT wearing a cape.)*
2   **KELLY: Scott, what's up with the cape?**
3   **SCOTT: All superheroes wear capes. And I have**
4   **transformed ...** *(Flips cape.)* **into a superhero.**
5   **KELLY:** *(Dryly, not impressed)* **Why?**
6   **SCOTT:** *(Dramatically)* **To save the world!**
7   **KELLY: Seriously?**
8   **SCOTT:** *(Halfway singing)* **Super Scott to save the day!**
9   **KELLY: Scott, have you reverted back to being a five-year-**
10   **old?**
11   **SCOTT: No, I'm a teen superhero.** *(Flips cape.)* **Super Scott to**
12   **save the day!**
13   **KELLY: I'm embarrassed for you.**
14   **SCOTT: That I cannot save you from. But a burning**
15   **building, a sweeping flood of waters, a flying dagger**
16   **headed your direction ...** *(Flips cape.)* **I can save you!**
17   **KELLY: Can you save me from my algebra class?**
18   **SCOTT: Kelly, do you really think a superhero could do that?**
19   **KELLY: Saving me from a burning building would be easy,**
20   **but from algebra ... I don't know.**
21   **SCOTT:** *(Flips cape.)* **Of course I can save you from algebra.**
22   **KELLY: You can?**
23   **SCOTT: Yes! Super Scott to save the day!**
24   **KELLY: How?**
25   **SCOTT: How?**
26   **KELLY: Yes, how can you save me from algebra?**
27   **SCOTT: Well, I ... I must keep my superhero methods a**
28   **secret.** *(Flips cape.)* **Like a magician ... we all have our**

1   ways! Super Scott to save the day!

2   KELLY: So, should I even bother going to fifth period

3   tomorrow? Will you stop the class from happening or

4   should I go ahead and show up in class and wait for

5   you to magically appear and save me from my final

6   math exam? Which I expect to fail.

7   SCOTT: Yes, you should go to your class tomorrow. But do

8   not fear ... *(Flips cape.)* I shall save the day!

9   KELLY: How?

10 SCOTT: And when you hear the fire alarm sound, run out

11   of the class as fast as you can. Run, don't walk!

12 KELLY: I thought it was walk, don't run. Anyway, do you

13   know what Mr. Jenkins will do to you if he finds out

14   you've set off the fire alarm? You will go from

15   superhero to student-in-detention so fast you won't

16   see it coming.

17 SCOTT: True. Then I shall arrive with a hall pass. *(As if*

18   *waving a pass)* Kelly, must come with me immediately.

19   No time for final tests. *(Flips cape.)* I am here to save

20   the day!

21 KELLY: That will never work. Teachers have seen that

22   game played so many times that they never allow

23   students to be escorted out of the room by another

24   student. Too many hall passes get stolen.

25 SCOTT: Then you must become violently ill during fifth

26   period. Lose your lunch in the trashcan.

27 KELLY: No.

28 SCOTT: Have a coughing fit that won't stop?

29 KELLY: No.

30 SCOTT: Fake a fever?

31 KELLY: No. Because once I go to the office and the nurse

32   takes my temperature that little lie will have been

33   exposed.

34 SCOTT: Toothache.

35 KELLY: They'd call my mom and she'd rush me to the

1   dentist. And my luck they'd find a tooth to pull.

2   SCOTT: Cut your finger. Bleed all over your desk and you

3   can go to the office and maybe get sent home for the

4   pain.

5   KELLY: I'm not cutting myself.

6   SCOTT: Well then, it looks like you're out of options.

7   KELLY: Wow. Some superhero you are.

8   SCOTT: My specialty is burning buildings and typhoons.

9   KELLY: Like that'll ever happen around here.

10   SCOTT: But if it does, I will be prepared! *(Flips cape.)*

11   Super Scott to save the day!

12   KELLY: *(Exits.)* Oh brother.

59. Litterbug

CAST: KATHY, NATHAN
PROPS: Crumpled paper, trash can, diaper, paper
SETTING: Park

1   *(At rise, NATHAN crumples up his paper, shoots it toward*
2   *a trash can nearby, but misses. He shrugs, then starts to*
3   *exit.)*
4   **KATHY: You. Hey, you! Come back here.**
5   **NATHAN:** *(Turns to KATHY.)* **Who, me?**
6   **KATHY: Yes, you. Get back here right now. You need to pick**
7   **up your trash right now. You saw that you missed the**
8   **trash can, didn't you?**
9   **NATHAN: Yeah. So?**
10   **KATHY: So? Is that all you have to say?** *So?*
11   **NATHAN: I tried, but ... but I missed! Guess I could give it**
12   **one more shot.** *(Picks up his trash.)* **And he goes in for**
13   **the winning two points ...** *(Throws trash toward trash*
14   *can.)* **And misses again. Let me try that again. And he**
15   **goes in for the winning two points ...** *(Throws trash*
16   *toward trash can.)* **Man, I'm bad. No wonder I don't play**
17   **basketball. I'm bad, aren't I?**
18   **KATHY: Yes, you are bad.**
19   **NATHAN: But enter me in a hot dog eating contest this**
20   **summer in the park ... I would make you proud.** *(As if*
21   *eating hot dogs)* **Forty-five, forty-six, forty-seven ... we**
22   **have a winner!** *(Raises his hands.)* **I won! I ate the most**
23   **hot dogs. Go me!**
24   **KATHY: That makes me want to puke.**
25   **NATHAN: I came in second last year.**
26   **KATHY: How exciting. Your talent — eating a lot of hot dogs.**
27   **NATHAN: Hey, I'm proud of it.**
28   **KATHY: Well, anyway, you need to pick up your trash and**

1   actually throw it in the trash can.
2 NATHAN: Who are you? The trash police?
3 KATHY: I'm a concerned citizen.
4 NATHAN: *(Offers his hand.)* Nice to meet you, concerned
5   citizen.
6 KATHY: *(Refuses to shake his hand.)* Aren't you the funny one.
7 NATHAN: I can tell a pretty good joke. Do you want to hear
8   one?
9 KATHY: Not really.
10 NATHAN: What do you get when you cross a chili pepper,
11   steam shovel, and a Chihuahua?
12 KATHY: I have no idea.
13 NATHAN: A hot, diggety dog!
14 KATHY: *(Glares at him.)* Who do you think will pick up
15   your trash if you don't?
16 NATHAN: *(Smiles at her.)* A concerned citizen?
17 KATHY: *(Puts her finger in his face.)* I hate litterbugs!
18 NATHAN: *(Picks up his trash and throws it away.)* Sor-ry!
19 KATHY: Thank you.
20 NATHAN: I still don't think it's that big of a deal.
21 KATHY: Not that big of a deal? What if everyone turned
22   into a litterbug like you?
23 NATHAN: Hey, and instead of taking out the trash every
24   night, I could just open the back door and throw it
25   out. Finished, Mom. Talk about easy.
26 KATHY: You are joking, aren't you?
27 NATHAN: I don't know.
28 KATHY: And I guess we could live in a filthy world if you
29   had it your way.
30 NATHAN: Mom says my room is filthy. Actually she calls it
31   a pigsty.
32 KATHY: I'm sure it is. Your poor mom. She's raising a lazy pig.
33 NATHAN: Hey, are you calling me a pig? *(Snorts.)* It's OK.
34   Maybe I am a lazy pig. Mom says I am. *(Snorts.)* I like
35   to enjoy life as it comes. Throwing trash away is

1   menial work. If I hit the trash can, good. If not, oh
2   well.
3 KATHY: And let someone else pick up your trash for you?
4 NATHAN: *(Shrugs.)* Sure. Why not?
5 KATHY: Let me show you something.
6 NATHAN: What?
7 KATHY: Follow me. Look right there.
8 NATHAN: Ooooh! A dirty diaper. Nasty! And it smells bad
9   too. Shoo wee!
10 KATHY: And how would you like it if someone threw their
11   baby's poopy diaper in your yard?
12 NATHAN: I'd get mad if they did that. I don't even like
13   babies. But poopy diapers? Nasty! Who would do
14   something like that?
15 KATHY: A litterbug like you.
16 NATHAN: I didn't do that.
17 KATHY: You were just as bad by throwing your paper on
18   the ground. These people threw a diaper on the
19   ground. As far as I'm concerned, you are all in the
20   same category.
21 NATHAN: I don't know about that. *(Points to diaper.)*
22   Because that stinks!
23 KATHY: And so do litterbugs.
24 NATHAN: Are you saying I stink?
25 KATHY: Yes.
26 NATHAN: Gee, thanks. *(Smells his shirt.)* Maybe I do a little.
27   But not as bad as that diaper.
28 KATHY: How about if I tear up this paper? Like this? And
29   then throw it on the ground? Is that pretty?
30 NATHAN: Not really. You're making the park ugly when
31   you do that.
32 KATHY: But what do I care? This is fun. And someone else
33   can pick up my mess. *(Continues to throw paper on the
34   ground.)*
35 NATHAN: Point made.

1 KATHY: Why should I care?

2 NATHAN: I said, point made! Look at the mess you're

3   making. And who do you think is going to pick your

4   trash up?

5 KATHY: A concerned citizen, I guess. But what do I care.

6 NATHAN: OK, I get it. I can now say I'm a recovering

7   litterbug. And I never want to go to that ugly place

8   again.

9 KATHY: *(Smiles at him.)* Good. Now you can help me pick

10   up this mess.

11 NATHAN: Me?

12 KATHY: Yes, you.

13 NATHAN: OK, but I'm not touching that dirty diaper.

14 KATHY: Me neither.

15 NATHAN: It really stinks.

16 KATHY: I know.

17 NATHAN: *(As they are picking up the trash)* I hate

18   litterbugs. And especially dirty diapers. And I don't

19   really like babies either. They cry a lot. Like this.

20   *(Demonstrates.)* I like dogs instead. *(Barks.)*

21 KATHY: *(Gives him a strange look.)* You have to pick up

22   after them, too ... if you know what I mean.

23 NATHAN: *(Shakes his head.)* Just can't get away from that

24   poopy stuff, can you?

25 KATHY: Afraid not. So, did you really eat forty-seven hot

26   dogs?

27 NATHAN: I did. Come to the park on the Fourth of July

28   and you can watch me beat my record.

29 KATHY: Maybe I will.

30 NATHAN: Hey, after we clean up this mess, you want to

31   grab some coffee?

32 KATHY: Sure.

33 NATHAN: Great! It's a date.

34 KATHY: It is?

35 NATHAN: I think so.

60. Surprise

CAST: CALLIE, PHIL
PROPS: Birthday card
SETTING: Outside of school

1   (*At rise, CALLIE rushes to PHIL and hands him a birthday*
2   *card and sings the "Happy Birthday" song.*)
3   **PHIL: Thanks, Callie!**
4   **CALLIE: Any big plans for your birthday?**
5   **PHIL: Oh, just dinner with the family tonight. Unless**
6   **someone throws me a surprise birthday party.**
7   **CALLIE: Wouldn't that be a surprise?**
8   **PHIL: It would.**
9   **CALLIE:** (*Throws her arms in the air.*) **Surprise!**
10   **PHIL: Here, I'll practice my shocked face. Do it again.**
11   **CALLIE: Surprise!**
12   **PHIL:** (*Looks shocked.*) **Oh my gosh! This is unbelievable.**
13   **You shouldn't have! Did that look believable?**
14   **CALLIE: Someone told you, didn't they?**
15   **PHIL: Told me what?**
16   **CALLIE: Don't play dumb, Phil. You just practiced your**
17   **shocked face on me. But honestly, it didn't look all that**
18   **believable.**
19   **PHIL: It didn't?**
20   **CALLIE: No. You'll need to work on that.**
21   **PHIL: But why would I need to work on that?**
22   **CALLIE: I just want to know who told you.**
23   **PHIL: Told me what?**
24   **CALLIE: Surprise!**
25   **PHIL:** (*Looks shocked.*) **How was that? Did I look believable?**
26   **CALLIE: Who told you? Because when I find out who the**
27   **snitch is, I'm going to hurt someone.**
28   **PHIL: Someone snitched? Who? About what?**

1 CALLIE: Your surprise birthday party.

2 PHIL: Someone snitched about my surprise birthday
3   party?

4 CALLIE: Why are you acting all dumb now? What you
5   need to do is keep practicing.

6 PHIL: What?

7 CALLIE: Your look of shock when you walk in the
8   restaurant with your parents and all your friends are
9   there.

10 PHIL: What? Really?

11 CALLIE: Let me show you how to do it. You say surprise
12   and I'll be you.

13 PHIL: I am surprised. Wow!

14 CALLIE: No, say surprise.

15 PHIL: Surprised beyond belief. I thought it was going to
16   be an ordinary family celebration tonight. Wow! A
17   surprise birthday party? For me?

18 CALLIE: Come on, work with me here. Say surprise. And
19   when you do that, I'll show you how to look. OK? Say
20   it.

21 PHIL: Surprise.

22 CALLIE: Not like that! But like this. *(Demonstrates.*
23   *Excited)* **Surprise!**

24 PHIL: *(Mimics CALLIE.)* **Surprise!**

25 CALLIE: *(Brings her hands to her face and opens her mouth,*
26   *speechless for a moment.)* **Oh, my gosh! You guys. I**
27   **can't believe you did this!** *(To PHIL)* **There. Think you**
28   **can do that?**

29 PHIL: I think so.

30 CALLIE: Well, you better get to practicing.

31 PHIL: OK.

32 CALLIE: Now, when I yell surprise, let me see your best
33   reaction.

34 PHIL: OK.

35 CALLIE: Surprise!

1   **PHIL:** *(Throws hand to his face.)* **Oh my gosh! You guys!**

2   **CALLIE: Is that the best you can do?**

3   **PHIL: I'm sorry. I'm still trying to get over the excitement.**

4   **CALLIE: What do you mean?**

5   **PHIL: I'm getting a surprise birthday party tonight. I'm so**

6   **excited!**

7   **CALLIE: You still need to work on that surprised look.**

8   **Let's try it again.**

9   **PHIL: OK.**

10   **CALLIE: Surprise!**

11   **PHIL:** *(Throws hands to face.)* **Oh, my gosh! You guys! I can't**

12   **believe you did this!**

13   **CALLIE: That was a little better. One more time. And really**

14   **try to look surprised this time.**

15   **PHIL: I am surprised. But OK. I'll do my best to show it.**

16   **CALLIE: Surprise!**

17   **PHIL:** *(Throws his hands to his face.)* **Oh my gosh! You guys!**

18   **I can't believe you did this! You guys are so awesome!**

19   **CALLIE: That'll do. Maybe they'll believe you were**

20   **surprised. We can only hope so. But I still want to**

21   **know who told you.**

22   **PHIL: Who told me?**

23   **CALLIE: Yes! Who told you about the surprise birthday**

24   **party? Because when I find out, I'm going to ...** *ooooh!*

25   **Someone is going to pay. So, who told you?**

26   **PHIL: You.**

27   **CALLIE: What?**

28   **PHIL: You.**

29   **CALLIE: Me? But ... ?**

30   **PHIL: I just said I was having dinner with my family**

31   **tonight. Unless someone threw me a surprise**

32   **birthday party. But I was just wishing. Hoping. I**

33   **didn't know I was really getting one.**

34   **CALLIE: You didn't?**

35   **PHIL: No. And I'm so excited!**

1　CALLIE: You mean, *I'm* the one who told you?
2　PHIL: Yes. Do you want me to practice my shocked look
3　　again?
4　CALLIE: It was me? Me? I'm the one?!
5　PHIL: Say surprise and I'll do my best this time. No one
6　　will ever know I know anything about it. Come on.
7　　Say surprise.
8　CALLIE: Surprise.
9　PHIL: *(Hands to his face.)* Oh my gosh! You guys! I can't
10　　believe this! I'm shocked! I don't know what to say!
11　　You guys! You are all so awesome! *(Smiles.)* How was
12　　that?
13　CALLIE: Great. Just great.

61. Star Trek Dreams

CAST: CARLA, JACOB
PROPS: Cell phone
SETTING: The front porch at Jacob's house

1 **CARLA: Jacob, we need to talk.**

2 **JACOB: What did I do now?**

3 **CARLA: Try what did I *not* do now.**

4 **JACOB: I don't have a clue. So why don't you enlighten me.**

5 **CARLA: You were supposed to pick me up from the band**
6   **hall at five, then we were meeting Chris and Jess at the**
7   **movies.**

8 **JACOB: Oh yeah! I forgot.**

9 **CARLA: I called your cell twenty-seven times.**

10 **JACOB: *(Looks at his phone.)* Yep. Twenty-seven missed**
11   **phone calls. Sorry. My phone was on silent.**

12 **CARLA: So where were you?**

13 **JACOB: Uh ...**

14 **CARLA: Tell me! What was so important that you forgot our**
15   **date? For the second time this week, I might add. Last**
16   **time you supposedly fell asleep.**

17 **JACOB: It's true. I fell asleep and missed thirty-two phone**
18   **calls.**

19 **CARLA: I only called you twice, Jacob.**

20 **JACOB: Hey, I'm a popular guy. What can I say?**

21 **CARLA: So?**

22 **JACOB: So, I'm sorry.**

23 **CARLA: So where were you?**

24 **JACOB: You want the truth?**

25 **CARLA: Of course I want the truth. Duh!**

26 **JACOB: I fell asleep.**

27 **CARLA: Again?**

28 **JACOB: I don't know what happened. I laid down on the**

1   couch to watch a rerun of *Star Trek* and the next
2   thing I know, I'm out like a light. Dreaming I was on
3   the Starship Enterprise, exploring new worlds,
4   seeking new life and civilizations ... to boldly go
5   where no man has gone before.
6 CARLA: Stop lying to me.
7 JACOB: I'm not! Then I woke up and Mom called me to
8   dinner and I never even remembered the whole pick
9   you up from band and go to the movies with Chris
10   and Jess date.
11 CARLA: I don't believe you.
12 JACOB: Do you want me to call my mom? She'll tell you it's
13   true.
14 CARLA: Well, I guess I'm just not that important to you if
15   you can't remember the plans we make.
16 JACOB: I think I'm just a sleepyhead. I'm sorry, Carla. Will
17   you forgive me?
18 CARLA: Maybe.
19 JACOB: Maybe?
20 CARLA: Maybe if you can remember what we have
21   planned for tomorrow night.
22 JACOB: *(Yawns.)* If I can remember?
23 CARLA: That's right. Or would you rather take a nap
24   instead?
25 JACOB: *(Yawns.)* No, no. I can remember what our plans
26   are for tomorrow night.
27 CARLA: Then tell me.
28 JACOB: You want me to tell you? Why? Because you can't
29   remember?
30 CARLA: No, because I don't think you remember and I
31   want to hear you say it. You just sleep through all our
32   conversations, don't you?
33 JACOB: That's not true, Carla.
34 CARLA: Then tell me.
35 JACOB: You know, I don't like being tested.

1   CARLA: And I don't like to be stood up while you dream
2   about *Star Trek* adventures.
3   JACOB: But those are some good dreams. To boldly go
4   where no man has gone before. Awesome stuff!
5   CARLA: You're not going to tell me, are you?
6   JACOB: Can we just drop all this and make up and move
7   on?
8   CARLA: Sure, when you tell me what our plans are for
9   tomorrow night.
10 JACOB: Because you forgot! And you're hoping I'll tell you
11   so it'll jog your memory.
12 CARLA: That's not true and you know it. Jacob, if you
13   know, just tell me and I'll quit accusing you of
14   sleeping through our dates and our conversations.
15 JACOB: Look, Carla, I remember our plans for tomorrow
16   night. You just be ready and I'll be there.
17 CARLA: *(Shakes her head.)* You're such a liar.
18 JACOB: I'm not lying!
19 CARLA: So, you honestly remember what we have planned
20   for tomorrow?
21 JACOB: Yes I do.
22 CARLA: And you remember what time this is happening?
23 JACOB: Absolutely.
24 CARLA: And where it is happening?
25 JACOB: Absolutely. How could I forget?
26 CARLA: I'm so glad you didn't forget.
27 JACOB: So am I!
28 CARLA: And I hope you'll enjoy your evening alone.
29 JACOB: What? Why?
30 CARLA: Because we didn't have anything planned for
31   tomorrow night, you dummy.
32 JACOB: We didn't?
33 CARLA: I was testing you!
34 JACOB: *(Yawns.)* This conversation is exhausting. I think I
35   need a nap.

1   **CARLA: Perfect. Now you can go back to your *Star Trek***
2   **dreams and sleep your life away for all I care.** *(She*
3   *stomps off.)*
4   **JACOB: Wait! I remember now! We didn't have any plans**
5   **for tomorrow night!** *(Throws arms up in the air.)* **Girls.**
6   *(Yawns.)* **Oh, well. Guess I'll have a little extra TV**
7   **time.** *(As he exits)* **The earth has survived World War**
8   **III and now we move on to explore the stars. To go**
9   **where no man has gone before.**

62. Tone Deaf

CAST: SKYLER, CALEB
SETTING: Outside of school

1 **SKYLER: Guess who's trying out for *American Idol?***
2 **CALEB: Who?**
3 **SKYLER:** *(Sings badly.)* **"And I ... I ... I ... will always love you!"**
4 **CALEB: Ouch.**
5 **SKYLER: What do you mean, *ouch?***
6 **CALEB: Ouch, you hurt my ears.**
7 **SKYLER: No I didn't. You're just jealous.**
8 **CALEB: Seriously? You're trying out for *American Idol?***
9 **SKYLER: I am. This summer when they show up for**
10 **auditions, I'll be there. Just give me that yellow ticket to**
11 **Hollywood.**
12 **CALEB: And what if you're one of those people who runs out**
13 **of the room crying because they tell you you're awful?**
14 **SKYLER: That wouldn't happen because I'm good.**
15 **CALEB: Who said?**
16 **SKYLER: Everyone. My mom, my sister, my boyfriend ...**
17 **CALEB: Have you ever had voice lessons?**
18 **SKYLER: No. And I don't need them. I'm a natural. It runs in**
19 **the family.**
20 **CALEB: Oh, really? Your sister sings, too?**
21 **SKYLER: Uh-huh. Last year she was one of the nuns in *The***
22 ***Sound of Music.* *(Sings badly.)* **"How do you solve a**
23 **problem like Maria? How do you catch a cloud and pin**
24 **it down?"**
25 **CALEB: Wow. That's uh ... just wow. So, do you think your**
26 **sister is a good singer?**
27 **SKYLER: She's a wonderful singer. Now granted she was**
28 **only the understudy for all the nuns in case anyone got**
29 **sick, but someone did and she was there and had all**

1 the lines and songs memorized and ready to fill in.
2 Of course they did tell her to sing quietly and they did
3 use a voiceover ... but I think it was only because she
4 had a scratchy throat from all the rehearsing.
5 CALEB: I see. So, your sister thinks she can sing, too?
6 SKYLER: She can. She's awesome! Being the older sister,
7 she sang to me all the time when I was a kid. I think
8 that's why I love to sing so much. I remember her
9 teaching me so many songs. Oh, she had such a
10 beautiful voice. *(Sings.)* "Mary had a little lamb, little
11 lamb, little lamb. Mary had a little lamb, its fleece
12 was white as snow."
13 CALEB: Wow.
14 SKYLER: Good, huh?
15 CALEB: I didn't say that.
16 SKYLER: And she used to sing me this one. *(Sings.)*
17 "Twinkle, twinkle little star, how I wonder what you
18 are. Up above the world so high, like a diamond in
19 the sky – "
20 CALEB: Stop! Please.
21 SKYLER: What? You don't like my singing?
22 CALEB: How do I say this?
23 SKYLER: Say it!
24 CALEB: You're horrible!
25 SKYLER: I am not. I'm a great singer.
26 CALEB: No. Honestly, I think you're tone deaf.
27 SKYLER: No, I think *you're* the one who's tone deaf.
28 CALEB: Skyler, you weren't even on key.
29 SKYLER: How do you know? Are you in choir?
30 CALEB: No, but I have a good enough ear to know what
31 sounds good and what sounds painful. And your
32 singing is painful.
33 SKYLER: No! The judges are going to be blown away by my
34 singing.
35 CALEB: And I think you're going to hear, "Dude, that was

1   horrible!"
2 SKYLER: I'm not a dude.
3 CALEB: That one judge calls everyone a dude.
4 SKYLER: No, he'll say, "Dude, it's a yes for me."
5 CALEB: Skyler, do you want me to go with you to your
6   auditions?
7 SKYLER: Sure. You want to?
8 CALEB: I think you'll need me.
9 SKYLER: Why? So I have someone to run through the halls
10   with me as I scream, "I'm going to Hollywood!"
11 CALEB: No, not for that.
12 SKYLER: Then for what?
13 CALEB: My shoulder.
14 SKYLER: Your shoulder?
15 CALEB: For you to cry on. I'll be there for you, Skyler. It's
16   OK. Don't worry about what all your friends say when
17   your audition airs on TV. Just tell them you did it as a
18   joke and you meant to sound that bad.
19 SKYLER: Caleb, the only reason I'd need you there with
20   me at the auditions is to congratulate me. Because
21   I'm gong to walk in that room and let the judges have
22   it! I'm singing "I Will Always Love You" by Whitney
23   Houston. *(Bursts out.)* "And I ... I ... I ... will always love
24   you" *(CALEB covers his ears and shakes his head as she*
25   *continues to sing.)*

About the Author

Laurie Allen was drawn to the theatre while performing plays under the legendary drama instructor, Jerry P. Worsham, at Snyder High School. In this small West Texas town, advancing to and winning the State UIL One-Act Competition in Austin was a goal often achieved. The drama department was hugely supported by the community and earned a reputation of respect and awe as they brought home many awards and first place trophies.

Following this experience, Laurie decided to try her hand at writing plays. Her first play, "Gutter Girl," won the Indian River Players Festival of One-Act Plays Competition. With that, she was hooked, knowing she had found her place in the theatre. Now, more than twenty-five of her plays have been published by various publishing companies. Her plays have been performed at many theatres including The Gettysburg College, The Globe of the Great Southwest, The American Theatre of Actors, and the Paw Paw Village Players. Her plays for teens have enjoyed wide success with many going all the way to national speech and forensics competitions.

Laurie Allen may be contacted at txplaywright@aol.com.

Order Form

Meriwether Publishing Ltd.
PO Box 7710
Colorado Springs, CO 80933-7710
Phone: 800-937-5297 Fax: 719-594-9916
Website: www.meriwether.com

Please send me the following books:

_____ **62 Comedy Duet Scenes for Teens**   **$17.95**
#BK-B332
by Laurie Allen
More real-life situations for laughter

_____ **Sixty Comedy Duet Scenes for Teens**   **$17.95**
#BK-B302
by Laurie Allen
Real-life situations for laughter

_____ **Thirty Short Comedy Plays for Teens**   **$17.95**
#BK-B292
by Laurie Allen
Plays for a variety of cast sizes

_____ **Comedy Plays and Scenes**   **$17.95**
for Student Actors #BK-B320
by Laurie Allen
Short sketches for young performers

_____ **Comedy Scenes for Student Actors**   **$17.95**
#BK-B308
by Laurie Allen
Short sketches for young performers

_____ **Improv Ideas #BK-B283**   **$24.95**
by **Justine Jones and Mary Ann Kelley**
A book of games and lists

_____ **Acting Duets for Young Women #BK-B317**   **$17.95**
by Laurie Allen
8- 10-minute duo scenes for practice and competition

**These and other fine Meriwether Publishing books are available at
your local bookstore or direct from the publisher. Prices subject to
change without notice. Check our website or call for current prices.**

Name: _____ email: _____

Organization name: _____

Address: _____

City: _____ State: _____

Zip: _____ Phone: _____

❑ **Check enclosed**

❑ **Visa / MasterCard / Discover / Am. Express #** _____

Signature: _____
(required for credit card orders)
    Expiration   *CVV*
    date: _____ / _____   code: _____

Colorado residents: Please add 3% sales tax.
Shipping: Include $3.95 for the first book and 75¢ for each additional book ordered.

❑ *Please send me a copy of your complete catalog of books and plays.*